PHASE STRUCTURE OF DHOLUO VERB SYSTEM

GALDA VERLAG 2019

ROBERT JOSEPH OCHIENG

PHASE STRUCTURE OF DHOLUO VERB SYSTEM

GALDA VERLAG 2019

Bibliografische Information der Deutschen Nationalbibliothek
Die Deutsche Nationalbibliothek verzeichnet diese Publikation in der Deutschen Nationalbibliografie; detaillierte bibliografische Daten sind im Internet über http://dnb.ddb.de abrufbar.

© 2019 Galda Verlag, Glienicke
Neither this book nor any part may be reproduced or transmitted in any form or by any means electronic or mechanical, including photocopying, micro-filming, and recording, or by any information storage or retrieval system, without prior permission in writing from the publisher. Direct all inquiries to Galda Verlag, Franz-Schubert-Str. 61, 16548 Glienicke, Germany

ISBN 978-3-96203-074-2 (Print)
ISBN 978-3-96203-075-9 (E-Book)

Originally presented as the author's thesis (MA), University of Nairobi, 2017

TABLE OF CONTENTS

Dedication—ix
Acknowledgement—xi
Introduction—xiii
List of Abbreviations—xvi
List of Figures—xix

INTRODUCTION

Background to the Study 1

Statement of the Research Problem 3

Objectives of the study 4

Research Hypotheses 4

Justification of the Study 4

Scope and Limitations of the Study 5

Definition of Terms 5

Literature Review 6

Theoretical Framework 7

Methodology 17

DHOLUO VERB ANALYSIS

Preliminaries on Dholuo Verb Analysis 20

Dholuo Phonology and Morphosyntax 24

Dholuo Morphosyntax 26

Morphology and Syntax of Valency 34

Summary 38

THEORETICAL ANALYSIS OF PHASE STRUCTURE OF DHOLUO VERB SYSTEM

Structural Design 40

T–Constituent 43

Negation in Dholuo 48

Summary 49

CASE ASSIGNMENT AND DERIVATIONAL MORPHOLOGY

Case assignment in Derivation by Phase Theory 52

Passive constructions 56

Antipassive constructions 59

Applicative constructions—the Benefactive 61

Summary 64

RESEARCH FINDINGS, CONCLUSION AND RECOMMENDATIONS

Research Findings 67

Conclusion 69

Recommendation 69

BIBLIOGRAPHY

DEDICATION

To all of us.

ACKNOWLEDGEMENT

First, I would like to thank my thesis supervisors: Prof. Helga Schrœder and Prof. Jane Oduor for their patience with me throughout this task, for their persistent and reliable advice, for their encouraging and supportive comments and criticisms that spurred me.

Special thanks to Dr. Maloba Wekesa who ignited my passion for syntax and the Generative Grammar enterprise in general right from my undergraduate syntax classes. On the same note, special thanks to Prof. Lucia Omondi and the late Prof. Okoth Okombo who nurtured my passion for syntax and kept my curiosity for it alive. And to Dr. Buregeya, thank you for believing in me. I am mostly indebted to the lecturers in the department of Linguistics at the University of Nairobi at large. To you all I say thank you.

In addition, I extend my appreciation to my friends and family who kept me going. I am forever indebted to you.

Finally, I would like to express my sincere gratitude to the University of Nairobi for funding my Master of Arts course through the Sasakawa Foundation scholarship from which this book is published.

INTRODUCTION

This study is a morphosyntactic analysis of Dholuo verb system in Derivation by Phase Theory. The study sets out to attempt to account for various aspects of the Dholuo verb system in a probe-goal relationship and feature based syntax proposed in Derivation by Phase theory. This theory has reduced major syntactic operations to two: Merge and Agree. The study particularly focuses on the relationship between tense, aspect, negation and the head verb. It also investigates case assignment, passive and antipassive constructions and the benefactive applicative in the Dholuo verb system in the proposed theoretical framework.

The research is qualitative in nature. The data for analysis are sentences in Dholuo collected from primary and secondary sources. The researcher's knowledge in language analysis and intuition as a native speaker of Dholuo offered primary data as well. Constant consultation with other native speakers was employed to avoid biases in data analysis.

The research findings show that Derivation by Phase theory cannot fully account for the linguistic variations of the Dholuo verb system without some modifications. In the case of case assignment, the study found that the assignment of nominative case as implied in the adopted theory could not account for such case assignment in Dholuo. This was because there was no tripartite agreement between the tense head, assumed to assign a nominative case in the theory, the subject and verb. As a result, there was difficulty in accounting for the subject pronoun and its case in Dholuo verb system in Derivation by Phase theory. In addition, the findings were that the assumptions held in the methodological analysis of passive and antipassive constructions could not be applied fully in the analysis of the unique behavior of the object in passive and antipassive constructions in Dholuo sentences.

The overall conclusion of this research was that there was need for some significant modifications and changes to the methodological analysis and assumptions held in Derivation by Phase theory so as to fully account for both the agglutinative nature of Dholuo verb system as well as the unique nature of the arguments to the predicate.

LIST OF ABBREVIATIONS

App	*Applicative*
Asp	*Aspect*
Ben	*Benefactive*
C	*Complementizer*
CFCs	*Core Functional Categories*
CP	*Complementizer Phrase*
DO	*Direct Object*
DP	*Determiner Phrase*
EF	*Edge Feature*
EPP	*Extended Projection Principle*
EXP	*Expression*
FL	*Faculty of Language*
Fut	*Future*
FV	*Final Vowel*
Hab	*Habitual*
HApp	*High Applicative*
***i*Asp**	*Interpretable Aspect*
***i*F**	*Interpretable Feature*
***u*F**	*Uninterpretable Feature*
***i*Neg**	*Interpretable Negation*
IO	*Indirect Object*
***i*T**	*Interpretable Tense*
LAPP	*Low Applicative*

Lex	*Lexicon*
LI	*Lexical Item*
MP	*Minimalist Program*
Neg	*Negation*
NegP	*Negation Phrase*
NS	*Narrow Syntax*
NTC	*No Tampering Condition*
Num	*Number*
Obj	*Object*
Pass	*Passive*
Perf	*Perfective*
Per	*Person*
Pres	*Present*
PRT	*Particle*
PSG	*Phrase Structure Grammar*
Pst	*Past*
Sg	*Singular*
Spec	*Specifier*
Subj	*Subject*
SMT	*Strong Minimalist Thesis*
***u*Asp**	*Uninterpretable Aspect*
***u*Neg**	*Uninterpretable Negation*
***u*T**	*Uninterpretable Tense*
***val*Neg**	*Valued Negation*
VR	*Verb Root*

LIST OF FIGURES

FIG. 1.1 The Interplay between FL and other External Systems. 9

FIG. 2.1 Dholuo Phono-morphosyntactic Analysis 21

FIG. 2.2 Dholuo Morphological Analysis 20

FIG. 2.3 Vowel Harmony System in Dholuo.. 25

1
INTRODUCTION

Background to the Study

The Chomskian perspective on language has shaped linguistic analysis of language ever since Chomsky (1957) argued against the adoption of Phrase structure Grammar due to its inadequacy to develop different derivational structures for passive and active sentence counterparts. In addition, Phrase Structure Grammar (PSG) couldn't account for re-ordering of constituents in a sentence yet speakers of a language usually re-order constituents during normal speech. Chomsky therefore pioneered what will later be known as Generative Grammar approach to language analysis. In the generative enterprise, language is an innate ability and a component of the cognitive faculty; Faculty of language (FL) specifically. Although PSG developed the basis of language analysis through re-write rules, Chomsky (1957) and subsequent publications aimed at investigating and accounting for principles that language employs in its operations. Chomsky (1965) thus came up with numerous transformations that could not only derive different structures for passive constructions and their active counterpart but also transformations that would account for deeper mental operations that account for how words are mentally re-organized and accounted for i.e. in Deep Structure before they are availed to the interlocutors i.e. Surface Structure.

Transformations proved to be quite cumbersome to syntactic operations and thus Chomsky (1981) argued for the introduction of Government and Binding Theory (GB) which focused more on principles and parameters that dictated the operations of a language. Although Government and Binding retained the notion of deep and surface structures, the theory introduced a schema that analyzed sentence in an IP form; case was assigned by the I in the IP and objects had to move to Specifier positions to be assigned case by I. Government and Binding theory was introduced as a modular theory which comprised of other theories such as the Binding theory which focused on description of anaphoric relationships and the Noun Phrase in general, the case theory which described morphological and structural case assignment in sentence structure. GB also included theta theory which assigns thematic roles such as agent, benefactor, and experiencer among others to the arguments of the predicate. Later on, GB was known as a theory of Principles and Parameters in that it could account for parametric variations in languages with the major variation being the pro-drop parameter. Haegeman (1994) explains that the pro-drop parameter distinguishes between languages that allow for the dropping of subject pronoun take for instance in Dholuo, the subject pronoun can be omitted because there is a morpheme that marks the subject on the verb. Hence Dholuo is a pro-drop language.

In 1995, Chomsky re-organized his theory to a more efficient approach to the understanding of optimal computational processes that are involved in the development of sentence construction. He calls this approach the Minimalist Program- a model of language analysis that regards sentence building as syntactic and morphological operations that involves processes such as numeration, merges and feature checking and finally spells out in the phonological component and the semantic component. In the Minimalist Program, case as well as other features such as tense and other properties of derivational morphology is checked using Heads such as subject agreement (AGRS) for Agreement of verb with subject and object agreement (AGRO) for agreement between verb and object.

Structure building procedure and representation in Minimalist Program still seemed too complex and thus Chomsky (2000, 2001) introduced the Derivation by Phase theory, a syntactic analysis methodology that focuses mainly on two Computational operations, Merge and Agree to account for the interplay between syntax and morphology in the analysis of language. Structure building is based on a probe-goal framework in a feature based system. Probes have uninterpretable features which are matched and valued with the interpretable features of the goal. Case is assigned by the verb and the tense marker (T).

This research will therefore focus on how the verb tense, aspect and negation is accounted for, how case is assigned, the derivation of passive and antipassives as well as the benefactive applicative constructions in Dholuo.

Background to the Language of Study

Dholuo ({*Dho*-language of} {*Luo-Luo* people}) is as a member of the Western Nilotic group in the larger Nilo-Saharan Language family. Although Luo people can currently be found nearly almost everywhere in Kenya, Cohen (1974) posits that Luo people are likely to have settled in the Luo Nyanza area around 1500–1555 AD. Having settled around Lake Victoria majority of the Luo people were fishermen and those who settled away from the lake practiced wheat, sorghum, millet, maize farming.

Dholuo dialects were initially geographically classified by Stafford (1967) as including the Trans-Yala Dialect (spoken in Ugenya, Yimbo and parts of Gem in Siaya County) and the South Nyanza Dialect. Later classification by Oduol (1990) emphasized the idea that the dialects could be grouped as Kisumu-South Nyanza (KSN) dialect and Boro-Ukwala (B-U) dialects. This classification covers a wider area and reduces uncertainty in the earlier classification by Stafford which had high *geographical spillovers* whereby some parts of the same location were argued to have two dialects e.g. parts of Gem had both Trans-Yala Dialect and the South Nyanza District dialect. Okombo (1997) points out that as much as these two dialects are highly mutually intelligible; the vocabulary used by members of one region is a firm basis for the separation. In her comparative study of variations in the B-U dialect Ochieng (2012) found out that the dialect itself also has sub-dialects such as the Ugenya and Alego sub-dialects. She illustrates using the example of the word casserole which is *ohuria* in Ugenya sub-dialect and *sfuria* in Alego Sub-dialect.

Okombo (1982) and Oduol (1990) agree that it is the KSN dialect that is usually taken as the standard variety of Dholuo and is thus used in in the rural setting where Dholuo is the language of the catchment area. The dialect is used in the media for example in Radio Ramogi FM, and TV. This research is based on the KSN dialect.

Unlike Bantu languages, Dholuo verb system is composed of free morphemes of tense, aspect, modals, auxiliaries and negation. The verb however, accepts bound morpheme of subject and object marking with only the benefactive marked morphologically in verb derivation.

Statement of the Research Problem

The development of Derivation by Phase theory in the study of computational processes involved in the construction of sentences brings with it new methodology to the understanding of how human beings not only speak and learn language but it also examines optimal computational processes in the language enterprise. Unlike in the Minimalist Program (MP) (1995) where there were several computation operations involved in the derivation of a construction of a language (L) i.e. Numeration, Merge, Move, Feature Checking, Derivation by Phase aims at reducing the computational burden by offering only two major syntactic operations: Merge and Agree. The Merge and Agree operations radically reduce the structure building process by doing away with cumbersome feature heads and feature checking adopted in MP. In the same spirit, this study investigates the optimal adequacy nature of the two operations (Merge and Agree) in accounting for Dholuo verb Morphosyntax with a kin interest in tense and aspect, verb derivation; (anti)-passive constructions, the benefactive applicative and case assignment.

Objectives of the study

i. To account for the pattern between Dholuo pre-verbal elements —such as tense, aspect- and the head verb in Dholuo sentences.
ii. To describe the structure of Dholuo applicative constructions in Dholuo verb system.
iii. To account for passive and anti-passive Dholuo sentence constructions.
iv. To develop and overall structural model of Dholuo Verb Phase structure.

Research Hypotheses

The study will test the following hypotheses:
i. Temporal relations of tense and aspect are probes in Dholuo Phase structure.
ii. The benefactive morpheme marker is a low applicative in the phase structure.
iii. Dholuo does not have passive constructions.
iv. The verb phase has multiple heads that act as probes.

Justification of the Study

The works of Chomsky on the study of language show that there are convincing grounds to believe that there are underlying mental process involved in the computation and general understanding of how language works. Consequently, the aim of this study is to explain the underlying computational processes in the morphosyntactic description of Dholuo verb system under the aforementioned theoretical framework and test how adequately the theory explains the properties and features of Dholuo verbs. Although several theories in the generative grammar enterprise have been used with the aim of explaining how Dholuo language computations work no study has been conducted using the Derivation by Phase theory to account for the Dholuo verb system.

This study would like to contribute to the existing knowledge on how Dholuo verb system operates in phases so as to account for verb morphosyntax and case assignment in Dholuo in a Derivation by Phase theory approach. The findings are likely to be useful to other researchers interested in the adopted theoretical framework as well as those interested in finding out the principals involved in the acquisition and learnability of Dholuo in general.

Scope and Limitations of the Study

This study will limit itself to the study of the Dholuo verb system. The main focus will be analysis of elements such as auxiliary verbs, negation, aspect and tense markers and how these elements relate to the head verb. In addition, the focus will be on the verb argument structure, how the verb selects and agrees with its subjects and complements. As a result of this morphosyntactic restriction, discussion of other branches of linguistics such as semantics and pragmatics in relation to Dholuo will only feature when highly necessary.

Definition of Terms

The definition of the following key terms was adopted from Crystal (2008):
Phase: This is a unit in a derivation that operates as an independent piece of syntactic structure.
Probe — This is a head that triggers move, agree and matching and valuation of features of its goal.
Agree — This is a formal relationship between elements in that a form of one word requires a corresponding form of another.
Applicative — A type of double object construction.
Phi-feature (ϕ) — This is a term for grammatical features of person, number,

gender and case. Feature is uninterpretable (uF) it does not add any semantic value to a lexical item e.g. feature number (Num) on a verb while a feature is interpretable (iF) it adds a semantic value to a lexical item e.g. Num on a noun.

Merge — This is an operation which forms larger units out of those already constructed.

Copying — This is a syntactic operation that makes a duplicate of a constituent in a given syntactic structure.

Anti-passive — This is a term used to describe a type of voice in ergative languages and it is an equivalent of passive in non-ergative languages.

Literature Review

A lot of research on Dholuo language using modern theories in linguistics has been done with the general aim being to develop a descriptive body of knowledge on the nature of Dholuo as a language.

Omondi (1982) adopts the Standard Theory of Generative Transformational Grammar to describe major syntactic structures in Dholuo such as complementation, pronominalisation, and possessive construction among others. Omondi shows how transformational processes involved in the theory are used in the computational process of Dholuo expressions in general. The analysis of complementation in Omondi (1982) offers a lot of insight into the understanding of how Dholuo verb selects and accounts for its argument in a transitive and intransitive construction in this study.

Okombo (1982) offers a detailed morphophonemic analysis of Dholuo structures and shows that the interactions between Dholuo word morphology and phonology is highly rule governed in a generative grammar framework. Elsewhere, Okombo (1997) provides a detailed grammatical analysis of Dholuo using the Functional Grammar Theory and clearly shows the constituent structuring of Dholuo expressions. In addition, it is in this research work that Okombo (1997) emphasizes the idea that Dholuo verb system has independent lexical items for tense and that it is aspect that is usually marked on the verb. This study employs the constituent order analysis by Okombo.

Oduor (2002) carries out an analysis of syllable weight and shows that there is a close relationship between syllable weight in Dholuo stress patterns as well as vowel processes of deletion and glide formation. In addition, Oduor reaffirms Okombo's (1982) vowel root lengthening—vowel doubling— process as one of the processes involved in developing a Dholuo syllable structure. Her research offers details on how to account for tonal nature of Dholuo verb system.

Ochola (2003) conducts a morphosyntactic analysis of Dholuo verbal system under the Minimalist Program. She offers valuable insights into the computational interactions between inflectional and derivational processes in Dholuo verb system and feature checking systems in the Minimalist program. Her study offers insight into the analysis of Dholuo verb derivation adopted in this study. In her morphosyntactic analysis of mood in Dholuo, Oluoch (2004) shows that mood in Dholuo is mainly expressed via structural modal auxiliary verbs that incorporate tone features. Oluoch affirms that the Minimalist Program adequately accounts for expression of mood in Dholuo.

Suleh (2013) investigates ambiguity of mood in Dholuo and adopts the Minimalist Program approach in her analysis. She concludes that tone plays a vital role in resolving the notion of ambiguity in mood in Dholuo and thus reduces the necessity of always placing Dholuo words in context for the purpose of disambiguation.

Theoretical Framework

The theory adopted for the purpose of this research is the Derivation by Phase theory (2000, 2001, 2004, 2007, and 2008). This an optimal theory to syntactic computations in that it champions for an economic approach to structure building operations.

Towards a Phase Based Theory

Haegeman (1994) explains that from a generative grammar perspective, the purpose of the linguist has always been to describe or account for what the native speaker tacitly knows about his language. This involves providing a detailed explanation of how the native speaker uses a set of mechanisms and finite resources to generate and interpret infinite number of expressions in his language. Derivation by Phase Theory, Chomsky (2000, 2001, 2004, and 2008) aims to answer the rhetorical question about language:

> *"To what extent is the human faculty of language* (FL) *an optimal solution to minimal design specifications conditions that must be satisfied for language to be useful at all?"* (Chomsky 2008:133–166)

Chomsky (2005) sheds light on the optimality nature of language by emphasizing that language should be thought of as an organ in the human body that interacts with other cognitive systems. This biological perspective of language is not new given that Generative Grammar was founded on that assumption. However, what stand out in this modern biological perspective are the three factors in the language design.

1. Three factor design in language
    i. The aspect of genetic endowment of language.
    ii. Experiences lead to variations in language use.
    iii. Language interacts with principles not specific to FL; external systems.

This third factor in language design is what Chomsky employs in an attempt to answer the question on optimality in FL. Chomsky (2004) proposes that since FL interacts with other cognitive systems outside its specifications, FL must satisfy an interface condition that seeks to reduce the burden Language (L) weighs on it. This is referred to as the interface condition and it states that:

2. Interface Condition

The information in the expressions generated by a language (L) must be available to other external systems including the Sensory Motor (SM) interface and the Conceptual-Intentional (CI) interface.

The interfaces introduce new elements to the general understanding of FL. However, these two interfaces are biologically indispensible. The S M interface is linked to the Phonetic component of L and the CI is linked to the Semantic component of L. Therefore, for an expression of L to be successfully generated, these interfaces have to be satisfied otherwise the derivation of the expression crashes. Pylkkänen and McElree (2006) argue for the interaction between Syntax and Conceptual intentional interface and state the principle that emphasizes this interplay. This principle argues that:

3. Compositionality Principle

The meaning of an expression is the meaning of its parts and how they are syntactically put together in a language (L).

Chomsky (2008:13-14) adds that the CI is an elaborate optimal nature of the interface conditions in that it resolves problems that hinder communication efficiency. For example, when syntactic operations of Merge lead to traces, how will language deal with the traces and gaps? To respond to this question, Chomsky (2005) proposes the C-I hypothesis which posits that:

4. C-I hypothesis

The C-I interface is a dual Semantic component whereby one component streamlines argument structure of expressions and the other component contains discourse related and scope properties for the interpretation of expressions generated by L.

Chomsky (2001, 2004, and 2008) argues that for language to achieve optimality in resolving the inherent computational and interpretive burden it has, language itself must be the optimal solution to those interfaces it interacts with. This assumption is referred to as the Strong Minimalist Thesis and it states that:

5. Strong Minimalist Thesis (SMT)

Language is an optimal solution to interface conditions that FL must satisfy. (Chomsky, 2000:96).

Chomsky (2000, 2001) adopts Marantz (1997) approach on the Lexicon (LEX). According to Marantz, the LEX is the source of the nucleic elements that enter the computation process. These basic elements enter the derivation carrying with them a bundle of grammatical features determined by the Universal Grammar (UG). Narrow syntax thereafter contains cyclic operations that will organize and map these set of atoms into the Phonological component linked to external systems such as the Sensory Motor (SM) interface and Semantic component which is linked to the Conceptual Intentional (C-I) Interface. This interplay between systems of FL and other external cognitive systems can be represented as shown in number 6.

6.

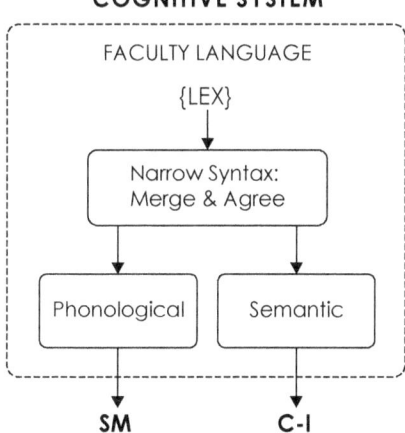

FIG. 1.1 The Interplay between FL and other External Systems.

Chomsky (2004, 2005, 2007, and 2008) refocuses on the computational efficiency and argues that NS is the sole engine of derivation of L. Therefore, when given the syntactic objects from the LEX, NS constructions a derivation (D) with the atoms, or syntactic objects as the heads of the construction and that NS has mainly two operations: Merge which comes free and Agree which is syntactically motivated. In order to reduces variations in attempts to argue for the SMT proposes a principle of uniformity that assumes that in most cases language processes are usually same except in the presence of compelling evidence. This principle states that:

7. Strong Uniformity Thesis (SUT)

In the absence of compelling evidence to the contrary, assume languages to be uniform, with variety restricted to easily detectable properties of utterances.

It is upon this line of thought that Chomsky (2000, 2001) comes up with an optimal theory whose aim is to reduce computational burden in the construction of expressions while still using finite resources adopted in the Generative Grammar Theory and supported in the Minimalist Program.

Derivation by Phase Theory

Derivation by Phase theory is an optimal theory that presumes that syntactic operations work out in units referred to as phases. It is an optimal theory in that it is a probe-goal framework in a feature based system. An expression (EXPR) is constructed using syntactic objects (SO) which enter the computation process carrying a bundle of grammatical properties and features (F). These SO's are heads of the construction and referred to as Core Functional Categories (CFCs). They include a light verb (v), complementizer (C), tense (T), and nouns (N). In the computation, these CFC's initiate operations such as Merge and Agree in a Probe-Goal relationship that ensures the configuration of the EXPR[ession] meets the interface conditions of the language (L). Once Merge and Agree are satisfactory, the chunks (=phases) are blocked to further operations by the Phase Impenetrability condition (PIC) and are mapped onto the Phonological Component through the SM interface and the Semantic Component through the C-I interface in a process known as Transfer. To avoid a lag in the processes, the assumption is that these operations are cyclic and simultaneous in nature. Finally the expression is Spelled-Out (S-O).

8. Phase impenetrability Condition

PIC states that in a given phase a with the head H access to the domain of H is blocked to operations outside a so that only H and its edge are accessible to operations.

Chomsky explains that phases are syntactic units that are propositional and derivational in nature. They are propositional in that a phase contains a complete argument structure as is the case with a Verb Phase (vP) and a complementizer Phase (CP) which indicates force and tense. Chomsky argues that it is mainly the verb phase and complementizer phase that should be considered as phases because they are also mobile and allow for syntactic reconstruction effects.

Mobility refers to the ability of *v* and C heads to move since they constitute a syntactic unit in the expression and that theta roles are assigned in the vP and CP is a full clause with tense and force indicators. Boeckx and Kleanthes (2007) add that the reconstruction effect of the vP and CP enables syntactic objects to move into the edge feature (EF) of the phase heads. The edge feature is the new term to refer to the specifier position of the heads. Legate (2003) demonstrates the evidence of an edge feature in passive and unaccusative verbs so as to demonstrate the evidence of strong phases. It is based on this feature that Chomsky (2001) distinguishes between strong phases which have the potential for movement and have an active EF.

Core Functional Categories (CFC's)

Chomsky (2005) proposes that instead of us relying on the pool of Lexical items in the Lex, we adopt a selection process that uses Core Functional Categories (CFCs) which guide the selection of syntactic objects and the mechanism involved in the computation as well. These CFCs are C, T, *v* heads and are responsible for the syntactic operations involved in creation and interpretation of an expression in a Probe-Goal relationship. A probe is a Core Functional Category such as C, T, *v* that seeks out, selects and agrees with its goal- a referential or a noun phrase within its C-command domain.

Fong (2005) points out that such a computational approach is an online processing that not only discards syntactic objects that have fulfilled their derivational process but also a unique mechanism that reduces unnecessary search while allowing merge of syntactic objects in the computational approach adopted herein. The probe and the goal enter the narrow syntax with a set of features that must be valued. It is this feature system that governs the relationship between a probe and the goal consequently inducing the major syntactic operations of Merge and Agree.

The CFCs act as Phase heads and enter into a probe-goal relationship with their targets. The assumption is that since only C (complementizer) and *v* (light verb) are phase heads, T can only be a probe as a result of feature inheritance from C. Adopting such an approach implies that categorical features of each syntactic category held by traditional lexicalism approach are abandoned and we adopt an atomic or bare root approach to the phase heads as proposed by Marantz (1997). Fong (2005) offers a sample lexicon of the CFCs and shows how they work with each other in the computational process.

| *v* |

The types of verbs that enter the NS from Lex include: transitive *v* {*give*}, such verbs in Dholuo include infinitive *tedo* (to cook), *chielo* (to fry) among others or unaccusative verb like *chuako* (to boil) and *turo* (to break). Radford (2009) also includes analysis of participles as examples of the verb. The light verb *v* (transitive) enter the derivation with the ability to select a complement phrase headed by V, Spec select N and value Case (accusative) through the operation Agree. The *select* is an inherent property in all probes. In addition, the transitive verb *v* enters the derivation with uninterpretable features (*u*F) such as person, number and gender which will be valued and deleted via the syntactic operation of Agree.

9. Transitive (v)
    $$\begin{pmatrix} \begin{bmatrix} \text{spec select } N_{[v\text{Value case (ACC)/select } V_{[VP]}]} \end{bmatrix} \\ \text{Per (?)} \qquad \text{Num (?)} \qquad \text{Gen (?)} \end{pmatrix}$$

The transitive verb *luongo* (to call) will thus have the uninterpretable features of number and person and have the ability to assign an accusative case to the goal that it will merge to i.e. a noun with the interpretable features of person and number e.g. *luongo nyathi* (calling a child).

10. Unaccusative (*v*) *yien otur* (stick is broken)

    $$\begin{bmatrix} v \text{ select } V_{[VP]} \end{bmatrix}$$

11. Unergative (v) Robert wuoyo (Robert is talking/speaking)

    $$\begin{bmatrix} \text{spec select } N_{[v \text{ select } V_{[VP]}]} \end{bmatrix}$$

| T |

Fong (2005) explains that there are two types of tense probes: T for tensed clauses and Phi-feature incomplete or defective probe for infinitival constructions. In tensed clauses, T selects (v) and values the nominative case but the defective T only selects (v). The defective T can only have the uninterpretable feature (uF) person.

| C |

There are two types of C probes: the declarative and the interrogative complementizer in Wh-questions. Both complementizers select T but only complementizers of a Wh-question have an edge feature or specifier position.

Feature System

Lexical items (LI) come from the Lexicon into the computation system having been embedded in them certain features and properties. Chomsky (20001, 2008) points out that the properties of the LI are to be referred to as its features. These features can be interpretable (iF) or uninterpretable (uF). These features include: person, number, case, gender, and in some probes an added edge feature. It is important to note that in probes these features enter the computation unvalued and it is through the operations agree that the features are matched with those of the goal and later on valued and deleted.

Pesetsky and Torrego (2007) echo Chomsky (2001, 2008) by pointing out that distinction between iF and uF is on the basis of a features contribution to meaning in the Semantic Interface. For example, in English, the feature number (Num) makes a semantic contribution on a noun and it makes no contribution on a verb i.e. two boys versus *two boy. Given that some features are unvalued and thus uninterpretable the bicondition that links interpretability to feature valuation states as follows:

12. Valuation-interpretability Bicondition (Chomsky, 2001:5)

A feature F is uninterpretable iff F is unvalued. Valuation and interpretation of features seems to re-introduces earlier-on debates on the role of semantics in syntax. Feature interpretability principles states that:

13. Feature Interpretability

A feature F is interpretable at SEM iF it makes a semantic contribution in the LI in which it appears, otherwise F is uninterpretable and must be valued and deleted.

Valuation as the distinctive role of syntax compared to semantics in the adopted theoretical framework is important. A transitive verb enters the derivation with unvalued properties such as case and a T enters the computation with properties for case as well. Syntax will thus valuate the case of the transitive verb as ACCUSATIVE and that of T as NOMINATIVE.

14. Transitive verb: [Attribute: Value] → [Case: ACC]

   T: [Attribute: Value]→ [Case: NOM]

Once features have been valued at the phase level, Chomsky (2001, 2008) proposes that they must be deleted through the process of simultaneous mapping onto the Semantic component and the phonological component of a language.

15. Deletion of uninterpretable features

The assumption here is that once valued, uninterpretable features are deleted.

Merge

Chomsky (2000, 2001) points out that Merge comes freely in the SMT approach. Merge is the operation that joins to syntactic objects (SO) together. The SO to be merged must be restricted to two for optimality in that the first Lexical Items (LI's) to be merged are the probe and goal whereby the probe is the head and the goal is the complement. Merge can be internal merge (IM) or external merge (EM). Both types of Merges are meant to satisfy the duality nature of the Conceptual Intentional Interface (C-I) in that EM caters for the argument structure and IM caters for the derived structure. Chomsky (1995) points out that IM will therefore leave a copy (-not at trace) of element being moved. Reliance on Merge as a sole computational operation eliminates the notions held in earlier theories such as the idea of a d-structure and an s-structure. Merge is checked by a condition which restricts Merge not to interfere with the SO's entering the derivation. This condition is known as a No Tampering Condition (NTC) and it states that:

16. No Tampering Condition

   Merge of X and Y leaves the SO's unchanged.

Merge yields syntactic relations of a set membership and a probe-goal relationship. Set membership consequently yields geometric structures of dominance, term of and c-command relations. Gallego (2007, 2010) explains that EM will merge a head with a complement and IM will merge a head with specifiers. In this case *chielo* (to fry) will merge with *rech* (fish). Gallego adds that for the specifier position to be availed, the head must project in advance so as to create the SPEC position for some SO to fill. Adhiambo will fill the specifier position of *v*.

17. Merge (a, b) = {a, {a, b}}.

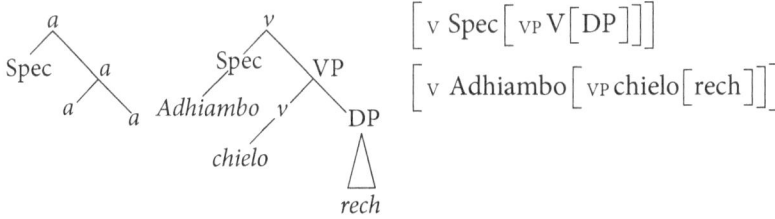

Agree

Agree is another complex operation that argues for the SMT. The assumption is that probes enter into the computation processes bearing uninterpretable features (*uF*) which need to be matched and valued against their Goals which have interpretable features (*iF*). Chomsky (2000, 2001, 2004, 2007, and 2008) argues that the agreement of probe and goal are controlled by the condition on agree which states:

18. Conditions on Agree
    i. Probe and goal must be active for Agree to apply.
    ii. Probe and goal should be local to each other.
    iii. Agree includes Matching and Valuation.

The activity condition states that unvalued or uninterpretable morphological features make SO's active. These features include: person number, (gender), and ability to assign accusative case. The transitive verb chielo (to fry) enters the computation bearing these features but they do not indicate value. Hence through the general operation of Agree, the verb and the goal-complement *rech* (fish) merge and the matching processes occurs so that the *uF* on the verb are made interpretable by the *iF* on the complement. The matching and valuation of *chielo rech* (to fry fish) can be represented as follows:

19. i. $\left[v\, chielo\, [\text{NUM}:?][\text{PER}:?][\text{GEN}:?][\text{Case:Accusative}] \right]$

ii. [N *rech* [NUM:SG][PER:3rd][Case:?]]

iii. [v *chielo* [~~NUM:SG~~][~~PER:3rd~~][~~GEN:?~~][~~Case:Accusative~~]]

iv. [N *rech* [NUM:SG][PER:3rd][~~GEN:~~][Case:?]]

Fong (2005) summarizes the Agree operations of Match and valuation as shown below:

20.

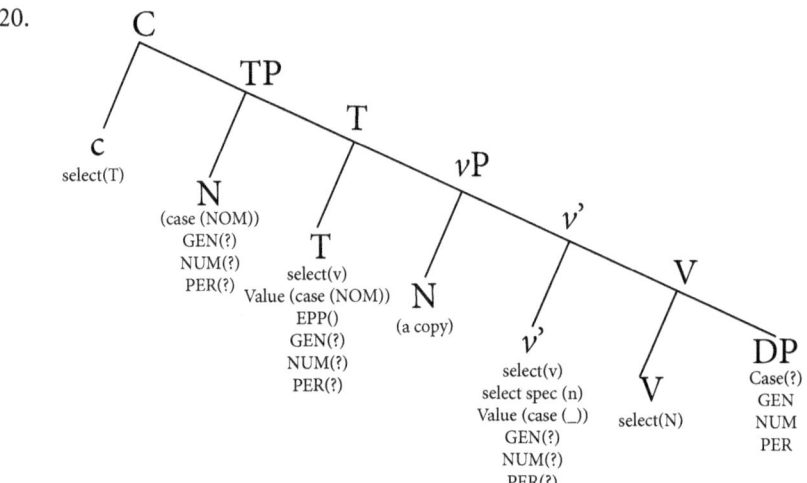

Transfer

After the operations, Merge and Agree, have been achieved in the respective phases, the operation Transfer comes into effect. Transfer is the operation that maps phases onto the Phonological and Semantic component to be spelled out. Radford (2009:327) echoes the following Chomsky's conditions on transfer are:

21. Transfer
    i. At the end of each phase, the domain (i.e. complement of the phase head) undergoes transfer.
    ii. After overall derivation, all remaining constituents undergo transfer.

Spell-Out

Spell-out (S–O) is the last operation in the computation process. Once the features of the merged syntactic objects (SO) have been matched and valued and they merged items have been transferred to the Phonological component and the semantic component, Spell-out gives the merged elements a phonetic form. Assuming that derivation occurs in phases, spell-out is also motivated to occur in phases with the first spell-out being that of the head verb and its complement in the *v*-Phase and onto C-Phase. The Spell out of the expression Adhiambo chielo rech (Adhiambo is frying fish) will be as shown below: Merge V chielo with complement DP rech. This is a complete Head-complement relation hence it is S-O. The subject Adhiambo is not yet S-O because it is in the Spec-*v*P position. The subject will then be raised to Spec-T in the CP phase and thus spelled out there.

22.
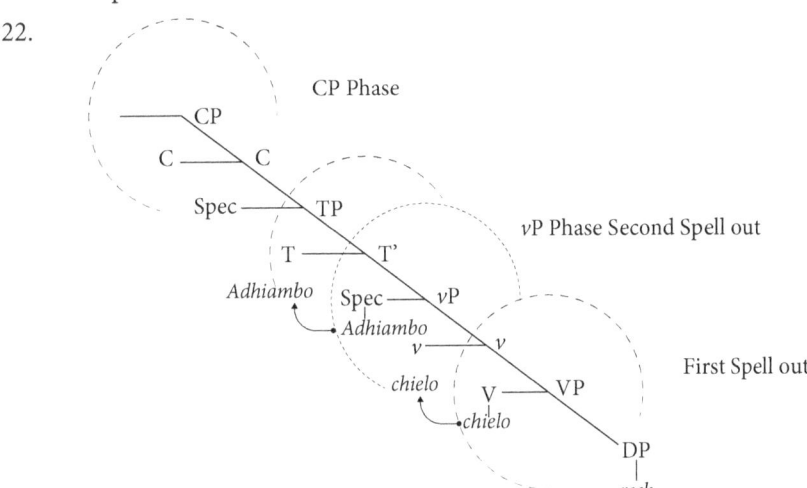

Methodology

This is study is a qualitative description of the Phase structure of Dholuo verb system in a Derivation by Phase Theory. The study describes the interplay between Dholuo verb and other variables such as Tense, Aspect and case assignment as well as verb derivation.

Data Collection

The main data to be collected will be Dholuo sentences. The data used in the analysis include secondary data collected from theoretical research already carried out on Dholuo Language as well as primary data collected via listening Dholuo sentences constructed in media houses such as Ramogi FM radio station. Primary data will also be generated by the researcher who is also a native speaker of Dholuo. The type of data to be collected will be terse Dholuo sentences and phrases.

Data Analysis

Data will be analyzed through the phase-based principles of the proposed theoretical framework herein. The verbs in the sentences will be analyzed on how they agree with their complements. The analysis will look at how the features of the verbs are matched and valued onto the features of the goal it takes. Passive constructions, the benefactive as well as case assignment will be analyzed from the sentences collected for this study. The accuracy of data analysis will be based on the researcher's tacit knowledge and intuition on Dholuo and verification from other native speakers whose opinion will constantly be sought after.

2

DHOLUO VERB ANALYSIS

Preliminaries on Dholuo Verb Analysis

The theoretical framework adapted for to this study is a morphosyntactic theory; an interplay between morphology and syntax. In their description of morphology in different languages, Haspelmath and Sims (2010:04) note that languages have different ways of expressing morphology. They argue that morphology can be expressed through morphological affixation, use of separate words or through implicit statements. Booij (2005:201) as well as Keenan and Dryer (2007:333) posit that morphology can be *strict morphology* in the sense that only affixes are used in a synthetic way or *periphrastic morphology* where by separate words are used to mark morphological operations. Dholuo verb morphology behaves differently; there is strict morphology as in the case of subject marking on the verb. There is periphrastic morphology as is the case in tense, negation and aspect markings. In addition, Dholuo employs phonological operations to account for morphological operations such as tense and aspect. Dholuo morphology can thus be represented as shown in figure 2.1.

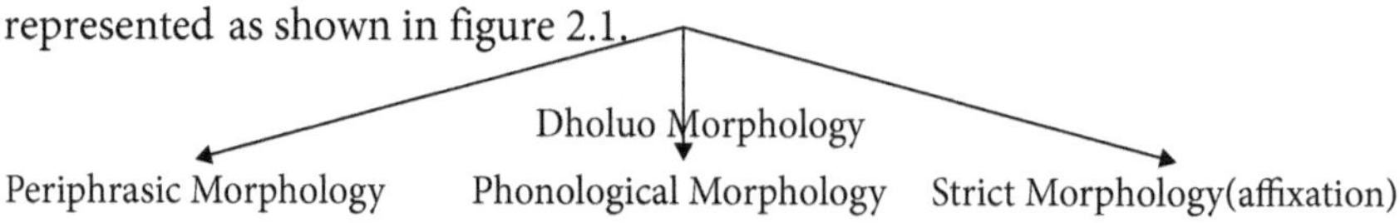

Dholuo Morphology

Periphrasic Morphology   Phonological Morphology   Strict Morphology(affixation)

FIG. 2.1   Dholuo Morphological Analysis

The interaction between morphology and phonology in Dholuo is quite intricate to the extent that certain morphological operations of tense, aspect and valency changing operations have to resort to phonology. Booij (2005:161) explains that in such aforementioned a morphology–phonology interface ensures that morphological structures are availed to phonology for the prosodic structures to be aligned as well. Phonological operations such as stress marking, tone shifting and vowel harmony are thus vital in Dholuo morphology. Consequently, these phonological operations tied together with the morphological operations influence Dholuo syntax, that is, valency changing operations. Haegeman (2006) explains that syntax will concern itself with testing hypotheses about sentence computations, diagnostics and analysis of sentence structures of languages with an additional systematic explanation of uniqueness amongst languages and computational processes involved. This tripartite interaction between Dholuo phonology, morphology and syntax can be represented as shown in figure 2.2.

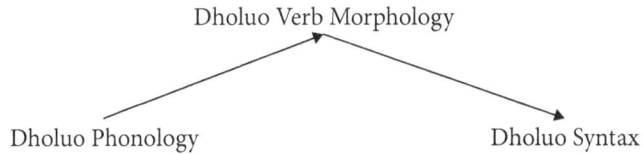

FIG. 2.2   Dholuo Phono-morphosyntactic Analysis

The above diagram shows that analysis of Dholuo verb morphology can be divided into two: a morphosyntactic approach and a Phono-morphosyntactic approach. Dholuo Morphosyntax will concentrate on how morphology—both periphrastic morphology and strict morphology (affixation)—interact with syntax while Dholuo phono-morphosyntax will investigate the tripartite interaction between phonology, morphology and syntax in relation to Dholuo verb system.

Subject Marking on Dholuo Verbs

Subject (*Subj*) pronouns in Dholuo are attached on the verb as prefixes. In the event that a proper noun is used, the subject marking on the verb is lost and the proper noun becomes the subject to the verb. The Subject prefixes are:

25.   **Singular forms**   **Plural forms**
        a—1st person (I)   *wa*—1st person (us)
        i—2nd person (you)   *u*—2nd person (you)
        o—3rd person (s/he it)   *gi*—3rd person (they)

Dholuo Verb Types

Dholuo verbs can be broadly classified as infinitives, modals, transitive verbs and intransitive verbs. The distinction between transitive and intransitive verb is realized in an argument structure because most verbs in Dholuo can be used transitively and intransitively with special modification on tone. This distinction is well illustrated in the sections head. Infinitives in Dholuo generally have a *final vowel* (FV) {-o} attached to the *verb root* (VR). However, a few infinitive forms lack the final vowel marker.

26. Dholuo Infinitive system:

   a) Paradigm of infinitive verbs ending with final vowel {-o}: {VR – FV}

chiel-o	*to fry*	tur-o	*to break*	med-o	*to add*	many-o	*to search*
nyiew-o	*to buy*	us-o	*to sell*	pok-o	*to peel*	chak-o	*to start*
kal-o	*to pass*	ring-o	*to run*	ted-o	*to cook*	wang-o	*to burn*
wach-o	*to say*	her-o	*to love*	penj-o	*to ask*	nind-o	*to sleep*

   b) Paradigm of infinitive verbs with no final vowel {-o}: {VR}

chiek	*to ripen/(food)*	yuak	*to cry*	dhi	*to go*
wuok	*to leave/to come from*				

Modals (Mod) in Dholuo can as well be divided into two: those that allow inflectional morphemes of person/subject and those that do not. The modals that allow inflection are *biro*, {-se} and *nyalo*. As a modal auxiliary verb, *biro* is equivalent to the English future tense auxiliary verb will. However, *biro* is also an independent head verb, that is, to come. The modal auxiliary verb {-se} is equivalent to the English modal auxiliary have as used in the perfect tense constructions. On the other hand, nyalo is equivalent to the English modal verb can. The modal auxiliary verb *nyaka* does not allow inflection for person on it. *Nyaka* is equivalent to the English modal auxiliary verb *must*.

27. Paradigm for modal that inflect for person and agreement:

   $$[\{Subj - Mod\} + \{VR - FV\}]$$

   a) *biro*–Future marker

a-biro ted-o	1st Per Sg-will cook-FV	I will cook
i-biro ted-o	2nd Per Sg-will cook-FV	you will cook
o-biro ted-o	3rd Per Sg-will cook-FV	(s)he/it will cook
wa-biro ted-o	1st Per Pl-will cook-FV	we will cook

u-biro ted-o	2nd Per Pl-will cook-FV	you (pl.) will cook
gi-biro ted-o	3rd Per Pl-will cook-FV	they will cook

b) {-se} perfective aspect

a-se chiel-o rech	1st Per Sg fry-FV fish	I have fried fish
i-se chiel-o rech	2nd Per Sg fry-FV fish	you have fried fish
o-se chiel-o rech	3rd Per Sg fry-FV fish	(s)he/it has fried fish
wa-se chiel-o rech	1st Per Pl fry-FV fish	we have fried fish
u-se chiel-o rech	2nd Per Pl fry-FV fish	you (pl.) have fried fish
gi-se chiel-o rech	3rd Per Pl fry-FV fish	they have fried fish

c) nyalo–modal auxiliary verb of ability

a-nyalo chiel-o rech	1st Per Sg-can fry-FV fish	I can fry fish
i-nyalo chiel-o rech	2nd Per Sg-can fry-FV fish	you can fry fish
o-nyalo chiel-o rech	3rd Per Sg-can fry-FV fish	(s)he can fry fish
wa-nyalo chiel-o rech	1st Per Pl-can fry-FV fish	we can fry fish
u-nyalo chiel-o rech	2nd Per Sg-can fry-FV fish	you (pl.) can fry fish
gi-nyalo chiel-o rech	3rd Per Sg-can fry-FV fish	they can fry fish

In the use of the modal auxiliary verb *nyaka* (must), the verb loses its final vowel and the subject pronoun prefix is attached on the head verb as show below:

28. Paradigm for modal that do not inflect for person: $\left[\{Subj-VR-FV\}+Obj\right]$

nyaka a-ted	must 1st Per Sg-cook	I must cook
nyaka i-ted	must 2nd Per Sg-cook	you must cook
nyaka o-ted	must 3rd Per Sg-cook	(s)he must cook
nyaka wa-ted	must 1st Per Pl-cook	we must cook
nyaka u-ted	must 2nd Per Pl-cook	you (pl.) must cook
nyaka gi-ted	must 3rd Per Pl-cook	they must cook

Case Marking in Dholuo

Haegeman (1994:159-164) points out that in languages with a fixed word order, noun phrases or pronouns are assigned case, the nominative case is assigned to noun phrases in the subject slot of a finite clause while the accusative case is assigned to noun phrases in the object position in sentences with transitive verbs. Dholuo uses a fixed word order of subject-verb-object

(SVO). Therefore, case assignment is similar to English case assignment paradigm. Haegeman adds that since the verb cannot assign an accusative case to noun phrases that it doesn't govern, then nominative case in finite clauses is assigned by the head of the clause which is the inflection head (INFL).

Dholuo Phonology and Morphosyntax

The relationship between Dholuo phonology and morphosyntax is inseparable in the analysis of the Dholuo verb system. Phonology plays a vital role in influencing both morphology and syntax of Dholuo in various ways. Oduor (2002) and Okombo (1982) discuss major phonological processes that affect the vowel. This study will, however, limit itself to tone, vowel lengthening and vowel harmony in this section.

Tone in Dholuo

Tone refers to variations in pitch that influence both meaning and grammatical relationship of a word (Ladefoged and Johnson, 2011:255). In Dholuo, tone marking on a word may indicate various grammatical aspects of the word. Tone in Dholuo indicates various tenses of a verb: present and past as well as the perfective aspect. The example below illustrates the variations brought about by tonal variations on the same verb in a sentence without morphological alterations. The tone pattern includes a high tone, a low tone and a down-stepped tone.

29. Á-lór-ó dhòt

    1st Pers Sg-close-FV door

    a) á-lór-ó dhòt—*I am closing the door* (present continuous tense).

    In the present continuous, the syllables start off with a high tone on the subject pronoun followed by a down stepped high tone on the second syllable and high tone on both the second and final syllable in the verb. The object *dhot* has a low tone.

    b) à-lôr-ò dhòt—*I have closed the door* (present perfect aspect).

    In the perfective aspect, the subject pronoun is marked by a low tone. The second syllable is a rising-falling tone and the final vowel on the verb is a low tone. The object *dhot* is marked with a low tone as well.

Vowel Lengthening

Odhiambo (1981) argues for the reciprocity between vowel length and stress and points that the two phonological processes seem to influence each other simultaneously. We would like to adopt the assumption that both stress and vowel length play a significant role in Dholuo morphosyntax without going into details of both processes in this study.

The lengthening of the subject pronoun on the verb manifests the past continuous tense of the verb form. Using the examples that show different meanings brought about by tone, we could add the following two examples in the paradigm to show a difference in meaning of the same sentence. Vowel lengthening is used when the past tense morpheme marker {ne} is not used to mark past tense.

30. a) á-lór-ó dhòt /aːlɔrɔ ðɔt/—*I was closing the door* (past continuous tense).
    b) wa-chiel-o rech /waːʧielɔ reʧ/—*We were frying fish* (past continuous tense).

Vowel Harmony

Vowel harmony is a phonological process that unifies all the vowels in a given word so that the vowels are all either high or all back or front vowels. Omondi (1982) explains that Dholuo vowel system has vowels that correspond with each other and can be contrasted as either high, front or back vowels illustrated as shown below.

31.

i		u
I		ʊ
e		o
ɛ		ɔ
	a	

FIG. 2.3 Vowel Harmony System in Dholuo (Omondi 1982:17)

Vowel harmony in Dholuo influences syntax of valency by changing transitive verbs to intransitive forms. There are two ways of valency altering when it comes to antipassives. The first case is where the verb undergoes internal morphological change and the other ways is through vowel harmony as illustrated herein.

32.	English	Transitive form		Intransitive form	
	To drink	madh-o	/maðɔ/	metho	/meƟo/
	To arrange	pang-o	/paŋgɔ/	pengo	/peŋgo/
	To get	yud-o	/jʊdɔ/	yuto	/juto/
	To pay	chul-o	/ʧʊlo/	chudo	/ʧudo/

Some verbs that lose transitivity via tongue root features variation without internal morphological change to the verb root include:

33.	English	Transitive form		Intransitive form	
	To peel	pok-o	/pɔkɔ/	poko	/poko/
	To remove	gol-o	/gɔlɔ/	golo	/golo/

In its transitive state, the verb poko (to peel) takes an object but in its antipassive state, it loses the object as shown below and the vowel system changes.

34. a) a-pok-o rabolo   *I am peeling a banana*   **(Transitive)**
 1ˢᵗ Per Sg-peel-FV banana
 b) a-pok-o   *I am peeling*   **(Antipassive)**
 1ˢᵗ Per Sg –peel-FV

Dholuo Morphosyntax

Dholuo Morphosyntax examines how periphrastic morphology and strict morphology (affixation)—interact with syntax. This interaction is discussed under the following headings: Periphrastic constructions and morphology and syntax of valency.

Periphrastic Constructions

Dholuo verb morphology accounts for notions such as tense, aspect and negation without involving morphological inflections but rather uses periphrastic markings. Periphrastic marking on the verb refers to the analysis of how free morphemes or lexical items account for inflectional paradigms of the verb in various grammatical contexts without changing its syntactic category. Dholuo periphrastic constructions include tense, aspect and negation.

Tense

Tense relates the time in which an even occurs to the time in which it is described. Lieber (2009) schematically represents this temporal interaction as shown below. Where, S represents time of speaking, E represents time of occurrence of the event being described. The disadvantage of adopting Lieber's schema is that it eliminates present simple tense.

35. Present   S = E
     Past   E before S
     Future   S before E

     (Lieber, 2009:94)

Although Lyons (1968:305) argues that there is a tendency during tense analysis in various languages to consider only affixes as tense markers and indicators, Levinson (2006:114) posits that not all languages have a rich inflectional system. Levinson therefore points out that some languages use calendrical units such as last year, two weeks ago or next time as well as diurnal span vocabulary such as today, now, later among others so as to locate the event being described in the traditional concept of past present and future timeframe. Dholuo verbs indicate tense through periphrastic marking.

Present tense form of Dholuo verbs is derived from the infinitive form of the verbs and there is no marking to show that it is present tense. The final vowel indicates infinitive forms.

36. Present tense paradigm: $\left[\{Subj-VR-FV\}+Obj\right]$

    a) a-chiel-o rech   1st Per Sg-fry-FV fish   *I fry/I am frying fish*
        i-chiel-o rech   2nd Per Sg-fry-FV fish   *you (sg.) fry/you are fry-ing fish*
        o-chiel-o rech   3rd Per Sg-fry-FV fish   *(s)he fries/(s)he is frying fish*
        wa-chiel-o rech   1st Per Pl-fry-FV fish   *we fry/we are frying fish*
        u-chiel-o rech   2nd Per Pl-fry-FV fish   *you (pl.) fry/you are fry-ing fish*
        gi-chiel-o rech   3rd Per Pl-fry-FV fish   *they fry/they are frying fish*

    b) a-nind-o   1st Per Sg-sleep-FV   *I sleep/I am sleeping*
        i-nind-o   2nd Per Sg-sleep-FV   *you (sg.) sleep/you are sleeping*
        o-nind-o   3rd Per Sg-sleep-FV   *(s)he sleeps/(s)he is sleeping*
        wa-nind-o   1st Per Pl-sleep-FV   *we sleep/we are sleeping*
        u-nind-o   2nd Per Pl-sleep-FV   *you (pl.) sleep/you are sleeping*
        gi-nind-o   3rd Per Pl-sleep-FV   *they sleep/they are sleeping*

Dholuo verbs allow the use of diurnal and calendrical elements to accompany the verb so as to clarify the relationship between time of event and time of speech. THese elements include sani (now) and koro (now).

37. Present tense with sani/koro

a-med-o pi sani	1ˢᵗ Per Sg-add-FV water now	I am adding water now
i-med-o pi sani	2ⁿᵈ Per Sg-add-FV water now	you are adding water now
o-med-o pi sani	3ʳᵈ Per Sg-add-FV water now	(s)he is adding water now
wa-med-o pi sani	1ˢᵗ Per Pl-add-FV water now	we are adding water now
u-med-o pi sani	2ⁿᵈ Per Pl-add-FV water now	you are adding water now
gi-med-o pi sani	3ʳᵈ Per Pl-add-FV water now	they are adding water now

The concept of past tense is marked by the pre-verb morpheme {ne}. The preverb element is followed by the verb usually in the present indicative or infinitive form as illustrated below:

38. Past tense paradigm: $\left[ne + \{Subj - VR - FV\} \right]$

ne a-nind-o	Pst 1ˢᵗ Per Sg-sleep-FV	I slept/ I was sleeping
ne i-nind-o	Pst 2ⁿᵈ Per Sg-sleep-FV	you (sg.) slept/ you were sleeping
ne o-nind-o	Pst 3ʳᵈ Per Sg-sleep-FV	(s)he slept/ (s)he was sleeping
ne wa-nind-o	Pst 1ˢᵗ Per Pl-sleep-FV	we slept/ we were sleeping
ne u-nind-o	Pst 2ⁿᵈ Per Pl-sleep-FV	you (pl.) slept/ you were sleeping
ne gi-nind-o	Pst 3ʳᵈ Per Pl-sleep-FV	they slept/ they were sleeping

Dholuo also uses diurnal elements to indicate different notion of the past tense implied. When the past tense indicators are used, the past tense morpheme marker {ne} becomes optional. This is illustrated by the following example:

39. Past tense lexical indicators

a)	nene	remote past	
	Nene a- med-o pi	Pst 1ˢᵗ Per Sg-add-FV	I added water (remote past)
b)	nende	near/immediate past	
	Nende i-med-o pi	Pst 2ⁿᵈ Per Sg-add-FV	you (sl.) added water (recently)
c)	nyocha	day before yesterday	
	nyocha o-med-o pi	Pst 3ʳᵈ Per Sg-add-FV	(s)he added water the day before yesterday

d) chon   *long time ago*
   wa-med-o pi chon   1st Per Pl-add-FV Pst   *we added water long time ago*

e) nyoro   *yesterday*
   u-med-o pi nyoro   2nd Per Pl-add-FV Pst   *you (pl.) added water yesterday*

Future tense in Dholuo is expressed using the modal auxiliary verb *–biro* {*–biro* + verb}. In Dholuo, the modal auxiliary verb used is {*–biro*} which is {*biro*} in its infinitive form. Unlike in the present tense and past tense where the head verb requires the *Subject* marker to be attached before the root verb, *biro* allows the Subject prefix to be attached to it so the head verb does not need the Subject marked on it. In speech, *biro* is usually contracted to "*bo*".

40. Future tense paradigm: $\left[\{\text{Subj} - biro\} + \{\text{VR} - \text{FV}\} + \text{obj}\right]$

a-biro tur-o dhot	1st Per Sg-will break-FV door	*I will break the door*
i-biro tur-o dhot	2nd Per Sg-will break-FV door	*you will break the door*
o-biro tur-o dhot	3rd Per Sg-will break-FV door	*(s)he will break the door*
wa-biro tur-o dhot	1st Per Pl-will break-FV door	*we will break the door*
u-biro tur-o dhot	2nd Per Pl-will break-FV door	*you (pl.) will break the door*
gi-biro tur-o dhot	3rd Per Pl-will break-FV door	*they will break the door*

Another future tense marker is '*ang*' and it also translates as will. However, unlike *biro* which takes the Subject marker from the verb, ang leaves the Subject marker in the verb root prefix position but deletes the final vowel, infinitive marker. This is illustrated in below:

41. Future tense paradigm: $\left[\{\text{ang}\} + \{\text{Subj} - \text{VR}\} + \text{Obj}\right]$

ang a-tur dhot	will 1st Per Sg-break door	*I will break the door*
ang i-tur dhot	will 2nd Per Sg-break door	*you will break the door*
ang o-tur dhot	will 3rd Per Sg-break door	*(s)he will break the door*
ang wa-tur dhot	will 1st Per Pl-break door	*we will break the door*
ang u-tur dhot	will 2nd Per Pl-break door	*you (pl.) will break the door*
ang gi-tur dhot	will 3rd Per Pl-break door	*they will break the door*

Future tense can also be indicated by use of temporal adverbs such as tomorrow, the day after today and among others. Dholuo marks future tense using the following adverbs of time as illustrated in 42.

42. Future tense and adverbs of time
   a) kiny — *tomorrow*
      a-tur-o dhot kiny — *(s)he will break the door tomorrow*
      wa-tur-o dhot kiny — *we will break the door tomorrow*
   b) orucha — *the day after tomorrow*
      i-ted nyuka orucha — *you will cook porridge the day after tomorrow*
      o-ted nyuka orucha — *(s)he will cook porridge the day after tomorrow*

Aspect

Aspect is a different way of analyzing internal structure of a situation being described by a verb. In his definition of aspect, Comrie (1976:03) distinguishes aspect from tense by emphasizing that while tense is focused on the relationship between the time of utterance and time in which the event is to occur, aspect is concerned with the internal state of the event, that is, is the event complete in itself or is the event not complete with less or no interest on time relations. Comrie goes ahead and distinguish between two major types of aspect: imperfective and perfective aspects. The perfective aspect regards an event as a complete situation without reference to the flow of time. Imperfective aspect on the other hand is the partition of a situation and regarding it in the chunks in which it is occurring. The imperfective aspect is further split into habitual aspect and continuous aspect. Based on this approach, we could state that the verb form fried corresponds to a perfective aspect while frying is an imperfective aspect.

43. a) *Robert fried fish*
    b) *Robert was frying fish*

The above example implies that we should view the verb fried as a single chunk of event and note that it is completed. We should consider the aspect in (b) as a series of small bits and pieces of the events of frying and not as a single event. There is no relation of time in discussion of aspect. Aspect in Dholuo is heavily influenced by Dholuo phonology, that is, tonal variation and vowel lengthening. The perfective aspect can however, be marked periphrastically with the same morphemes that mark tense. The morphemes {ne} and {–se} are used in similar fashion they are used in indicating tense. In the use of the morpheme {–se} to mark perfective aspect, the Subject marker is attached on the perfect aspect marker {–se}:

44. Paradigm for marking perfective aspect with {–se}:

$$[\{Subj-se\} + \{VR-FV\} + Obj]$$

a-se chiel-o rech	1st Per Sg-Perf fry-FV fish	I have fried fish
i-se chiel-o rech	2nd Per Sg-Perf fry-FV fish	you have fried fish
o-se chiel-o rech	3rd Per Sg-Perf fry-FV fish	(s)he has fried fish
wa-se chiel-o rech	1st Per Pl-Perf fry-FV fish	we have fried fish
u-se chiel-o rech	2nd Per Pl-Perf fry-FV fish	fish you (pl.) have fried fish
gi-se chiel-o rech	3rd Per Pl-Perf fry-FV fish	they have fried fish

The use of the morpheme, {ne} to mark perfective aspect has to introduce tonal variation into the analysis. This is because once {ne} is used, only tone can tell whether the sentence is perfective or imperfective since the morphological structure is the same in both cases. This is illustrated below.

45. a) **Dholuo sentence** — **Perfective**

ne a-achiel-o rech	Pst 1st Per Sg-fry-FV fish	I fried fish
ne i-chiel-o rech	Pst 2dn Per Sg-fry-FV fish	you (sg.) fried fish
ne o-chiel-o rech	Pst 3rd Per Sg-fry-FV fish	(s)he fried fish
ne wa-chiel-o rech	Pst 1st Per Pl-fry-FV fish	we fried fish
ne u-chiel-o rech	Pst 2nd Per Pl-fry-FVfish	you (pl.) fried fish
ne gi-chiel-o rech	Pst 3rd Per Pl-fry-FV fish	they fried fish

b) **Dholuo sentence** — **Imperfective**

ne a-achiel-o rech	Pst 1st Per Sg-fry-FV fish	I was frying fish
ne i-chiel-o rech	Pst 2dn Per Sg-fry-FV fish	you was frying fish
ne o-chiel-o rech	Pst 3rd Per Sg-fry-FV fish	(s)he was frying fish
ne wa-chiel-o rech	Pst 1st Per Pl-fry-FV fish	we was frying fish
ne u-chiel-o rech	Pst 2nd Per Pl-fry-FV fish	you (pl.) was frying fish
ne gi-chiel-o rech	Pst 3rd Per Pl-fry-FV fish	they was frying fish

The habitual imperfective aspect is marked in Dholuo by the suffix {–ga}. In the use of {–ga}, the verb retains its final vowel {–o} as indicated below:

46. Habitual aspect marker {–ga}: $[\{Subj-VR-FV-Hab\} + Obj]$

a) a-chiel-o-ga rech	1st Per Sg-fry-FV-Hab fish	I usually fry fish
i-chiel-o-ga rech	2nd Per Sg-fry-FV-Hab fish	you (sg.) usually fry fish

o-chiel-o-ga rech	3rd Per Sg-fry-FV-Hab fish	(s)he usually fry fish
wa-chiel-o-ga rech	1st Per Pl-fry-FV-Hab fish	we usually fry fish
u-chiel-o-ga rech	2nd Per Pl-fry-FV-Hab fish	you (pl.) usually fry fish
gi-chiel-o-ga rech	3rd Per Pl-fry-FV-Hab fish	they usually fry fish

Negation

There are three preverb morphemes that mark negation in Dholuo. They include ok, kik, and pok. ok is the general negation marker. Kik is reserved for command sentences, imperatives. On the other hand, pok on the other hand is used to make the English equivalent of not yet.

In present tense constructions, the use of ok affects the final vowel, that is, the infinitive marker is deleted and ok is only placed before the verb:

47. Negation paradigm with ok in present tense: $[ok + \{Subj - VR\} + Obj]$

ok a-chiel rech	Neg 1st Per Sg-fry fish	I don't fry/I am not frying fish
ok i-chiel rech	Neg 2nd Per Sg-fry fish	you don't fry/ are not frying fish
ok o-chiel rech	Neg 3rd Per Sg-fry fish	(s)he doesn't fries/ is not frying fish
ok wa-chiel rech	Neg 1st Per Pl-fry fish	we don't fry/we are not frying fish
ok u-chiel rech	Neg 2nd Per Pl-fry fish	you (pl.) don't fry/are not frying fish
ok gi-chiel rech	Neg 3rd Per Pl-fry fish	they don't fry/ are not frying fish

In past tense sentences, ok influences the head verb in two ways. Ok can be used with the verb keeping the final vowel {-o} to denote negation of past continuous tense or there is the deletion of the final vowel {-o} in constructions as shown below.

48. Negation in past tense.

a) Negation paradigm with -ok- in present tense: $[ne + ok \{Subj - VR\} + Obj]$

ne ok a-chiel rech	Pst Neg 1st Per Sg-fry fish	I was not frying fish
ne ok i-chiel rech	Pst Neg 2nd Per Sg-fry fish	you (sg.) were not frying fish
ne ok o-chiel rech	Pst Neg 3rd Per Sg-fry fish	(s)he was not frying fish
ne ok wa-chiel rech	Pst Neg 1st Per Pl-fry fish	we were not frying fish
ne ok u-chiel rech	Pst Neg 2nd Per Pl-fry fish	you (pl.) were not frying fish
ne ok gi-chiel rech	Pst Neg 3rd Per Pl-fry fish	they were not frying fish

b) Negation paradigm with -ok- in present tense: $[ne + ok \{Subj - VR - FV\} + Obj]$

ne ok a-chiel-o rech	Pst Neg 1st Per Sg-fry fish	I didn't fry fish
ne ok i-chiel-o rech	Pst Neg 2nd Per Sg-fry fish	you didn't fry fish

ne ok o-chiel-o rech	Pst Neg 3rd Per Sg-fry fish	(s)he didn't fry fish
ne ok wa-chiel-o rech	Pst Neg 1st Per Pl-fry fish	we didn't fry fish
ne ok u-chiel-o rech	Pst Neg 2nd Per Pl-fry fish	you (pl.) didn't fry fish
ne ok gi-chiel-o rech	Pst Neg 3rd Per Pl-fry fish	they didn't fry fish

In future tense, the negative marker ok precedes the modal auxiliary verb {-biro}. Unlike in positive future sentences where the modal auxiliary *biro* is contracted to "*bo*" in negative sentences, the modal auxiliary is contracted to "*bi*" in speech.

49. Negation in future tense: $\left[\text{ok} + \{\text{Subj} - biro\} + \{\text{VR} - \text{FV}\}\right]$

ok a-biro ted-o	Neg 1st Per Sg-will cook-FV	I will not cook
ok i-biro ted-o	Neg 2nd Per Sg-will cook-FV	you will not cook
ok o-biro ted-o	Neg 3rd Per Sg-will cook-FV	he will not cook

In the derivation of imperatives the negation marker kik, the verb drops the final vowel and keeps the subject attached to it. The use of *kik* is equivalent to English negative imperatives like *don't sit here* only that in English, there are no subject markers in imperatives.

50. Negation with *kik*: $\left[\text{kik} + \{\text{Subj} - \text{VR}\} + \text{Obj}\right]$

kik a-tur dhot	Neg 1st Per Sg-break door	(I) don't break the door
kik i-tur dhot	Neg 2nd Per Sg-break door	(you) don't break the door
kik o-tur dhot	Neg 3rd Per Sg-break door	(s/he) don't break the door
kik wa-tur dhot	Neg 1st Per Pl-break door	(we) don't break the door
kik u-tur dhot	Neg 2nd Per Pl-break door	(you) (pl.) don't break the door
kik gi-tur dhot	Neg 3rd Per Pl-break door	(they) don't break the door

The negation marker pok is used to mark negation in the perfect tense. In the use of pok, the verb retains its final vowel, infinitive marker {-o} and the subject as well. The use of pok is as illustrated in 51.

51. Negation in perfect tense constructions.

   a) Negation in present perfect tense: $\left[\text{pok} + \{\text{Subj} - \text{VR} - \text{FV}\} + \text{Obj}\right]$

pok a-chiel-o rech	Neg Perf 1st Per Sg-fry-FV fish	I haven't fried fish
pok i-chiel-o rech	Neg Perf 2nd Per Sg-fry-FV fish	you haven't fried fish
pok o-chiel-o rech	Neg Perf 3rd Per Sg-fry-FV fish	(s)he hasn't fried fish

In past perfect tense, the negation marker has to combine with all the preverb markers such as ne for tense as shown below.

b) Negation in present perfect tense: $[\text{pok} + \text{ne} + \{\text{VR} - \text{FV}\} + \text{Obj}]$

ne pok a-chiel-o rech	Neg Perf 1ˢᵗ Per Sg-fry-FV fish	I hadn't fried fish
ne pok i-chiel-o rech	Neg Perf 1ˢᵗ Per Sg-fry-FV fish	you hadn't fried fish
ne pok o-chiel-o rech	Neg Perf 1ˢᵗ Per Sg-fry-FV fish	(s)he hadn't fried fish

Morphology and Syntax of Valency

Valency is the number of arguments taken by a verb in a sentence because those arguments have a role to play in the general meaning of the verb. Valency changing operations can increase the number of arguments required by a verb or decrease the number of arguments used in a verb. For example, a transitive verb may be changed to an intransitive verb when an argument is removed from it while an intransitive verb can be made transitive by adding an argument to it. Some common sentence constructions that employ such operations include: passive sentences, antipassive constructions and the use of applicative to mark notions such as the benefactive construction.

Passive Constructions

Passivization reduces the number of arguments taken by a verb in its active voice. Booij (2005:194) explains that the agent in the active voice is demoted in the passive construction by relegating it to a peripheral preposition phrases headed by the preposition by. Consequently, the patient/theme in the active sentence is given prominence as the shadow-agent in the passive sentence construction. THe tense of the active voice is accounted for by the auxiliary verb *be* which precedes the past participle of the verb in the passive voice. THis can be represented as:

52. Schema for English Passive sentences

   a) Active Voice: Subject + Verb + Object
      Passive Voice: Object + to be$_{\text{(tense)}}$ + Verb$_{\text{(past participle)}}$ + by Subject
   b) Active Voice: Robert fried fish
      Passive Voice: Fish was fried (by Robert)

In Dholuo, passive constructions are denoted by the prefix {o-} and {i-} on the verb. The prefix {o-} and {i-} indicate the internal state, aspect, of the verb whereby {o-} marks perfective aspect or completed state while {i-}

marks imperfective aspect of the verb. The subject is headed by a prepositional phrase headed by gi (by). In addition, Dholuo uses tone to mark present tense, periphrastic markers {*ne*} for past and {–*biro*} for future tense.

53. Dholuo passives in present tense:

   a) Active Voice: $\{Subj + VR - FV\} + Obj$

   Passive Voice: $\left[\{Pass\text{-}VR\text{-}FV\} + Obj + (gi + Subj)\right]$

   b) a-chiel-o rech   *I am frying fish/ I fry fish*
   1st Per Sg- fry-FV fish
   i-chiel-o rech (gi an)   *fish is being fried by me*
   Pass-fry-FV fish (by-me)
   Robert chiel-o rech   *Robert fries/is frying fish*
   Robert fry-FV fish
   i-chiel-o rech (gi Robert)   *fish is being fried by Robert*
   Pass-fry-FV fish (by Robert)

Dholuo passives in past tense are formed by the passive prefix {o–} attached on the verb. Consequently, the verb loses its final vowel {–o}. This is illustrated in 54.

54. a) Active Voice: $\left[ne\ \{Subj - VR - FV\} + Obj\right]$

   Passive Voice: $\left[ne\ \{Pass - VR\} + Obj + (gi + Subject)\right]$

   b) ne a-chiel-o rech   *I fried fish*
   PST 1st Per Sg-fry-FV fish
   Ne o-chiel rech   *fish was fried*
   PST Pass-fry fish

Active sentences are made passive by attaching the passive marker in the auxiliary verb biro and the verb loses its final vowel {–o}.

55. a) Active Voice: $\left[\{Subj\text{-}biro\} + VR - FV + Obj\right]$

   Passive Voice: $\left[\{i\text{-}biro\} + \{VR\text{-}FV\} + Obj + (gi + subject)\right]$

   b) a-biro chiel-o rech   *I will fry fish*
   1st Per-will fry-FV fish
   i-biro chiel rech   *fish will be fired*
   Pass-will fry fish

In perfect tense, the passive prefix marker {o–} attached on the perfect tense marker {–se} and the verb loses its final vowel {–o}.

56. Active Voice: $\left[\{\text{Subj}-\text{se}\} + \{\text{VR}-\text{FV}\} + \text{Obj}\right]$

    Passive Voice: $\left[\{\text{Pass}-\text{se}\} + \{\text{VR}\} + \text{Obj} + (\text{gi} + \text{Subject})\right]$

a-se chiel-o rech	1st Per Sg fry-FV fish	*I have fried fish*
o-se chiel rech	Pass-Perf fry fish	*Fish has been fried*

There is a close morphological resemblance between passive constructions and active sentences bearing the prefix Subject markers {i–} and {o–} for second and third person, respectively. However, the deletion of the final vowel and regulation in the use of the passive prefixes {i–} and {o–} is peculiar in the verb paradigm.

Antipassive Constructions

In antipassive voice, the transitive verb loses one of its arguments. Lieber (2009) points out that the difference between antipassive sentences and passive sentences is that while the argument in passives is demoted or ignored, in antipassives, the argument is completely deleted or lost. As a result, the transitive verb becomes intransitive. In most cases, Dholuo verbs are both transitive and intransitive.

In Dholuo, antipassives are marked in two ways: internal change of the verb root or by tone. Some of the verbs that mark antipassive by internal verb change include the following verbs in (57). The discussion on the vowel features relating to the examples below in (57, 58) have been discussed.

57. | **English** | **Transitive form** | **Intransitive form** |
|---|---|---|
| *To eat* | chamo | chiemo |
| *To pay* | chul-o | chudo |
| *To fry* | chiel-o | chiedo |
| *To boil* | chwak-o | chweko |
| *To drink* | madh-o | metho |
| *To arrange* | pang-o | pengo |
| *To get* | yud-o | yuto |
| *To open* | yaw-o | yepo |

Some verbs that lose transitivity via variation in tongue root features include:

58. | **English** | **Transitive form** | **Intransitive form** |
|---|---|---|
| *To peel* | pok-o | poko |
| *To remove* | gol-o | golo |

The sentences below illustrate the nature of antipassives in Dholuo:

59. a) a-madh-o chai   *I am drinking tea.*
1st Per Sg-drink-FV tea

a-meth-o   *I am drinking.*
1st Per Sg-drink-FV

b) o-gol-o pesa   *(S)He is removing money.*
2nd Per Sg-remove-FV money   *(S)He is removing.*

Applicative Constructions

Applicative constructions are valency increasing operations in a language. Applicatives include benefactive, instrument and locative. In Dholuo, the benefactive marker is indicated by the suffix {–n–}. The suffix allows for fixing the object suffix pronoun at the end of it.

60. Benefactive paradigm: $[\{\text{Subj-VR-FV-Ben-Obj}\} + \text{Obj}]$

    a) a-chiel-o-n-a rech   *I am frying fish for myself*
        a-chiel-o-n-i rech   *I am frying fish for you (sg.)*
        a-chiel-o-n-e rech   *I am frying fish for him/her/it*
        a-chiel-o-n-wa rech   *I am frying fish for us*
        a-chiel-o-n-u rech   *I am frying fish for you (pl.)*
        a-chiel-o-n-egi rech   *I am frying fish for them*

    b) i-biro ted-o-n-a nyuka   *you will cook porridge for me*
        i-biro ted-o-n-i nyuka   *you will cook porridge for yourself*
        i-biro ted-o-n-e nyuka   *you will cook porridge for him/her/it*
        i-biro ted-o-n-wa nyuka   *you will cook porridge for us*
        i-biro ted-o-n-u nyuka   *you will cook porridge for yourselves*
        i-biro ted-o-n-egi nyuka   *you will cook porridge for them*

Summary

So far, we have demonstrated that Dholuo verb system entails negation markers, tense/aspect markers subject markers and the object marking as well in the case of the benefactive. The morphosyntactic alignment of Dholuo verb system is linked with the phonological operations of the sentential elements. Thus, a wrong alignment will generate ungrammatical sentences or sometimes unintended meaning. In addition, a wrong phonological operation can also lead to a wrong or unintended meaning. Additionally, a given tone, vowel length or tongue root feature may generate unintended sentence form. The guiding principles in Dholuo verb system alignment can be summarized as shown below.

61. a) Verb roots (VR) always do not precede Subject markers.

      a-chiel-o rech   *I am frying fish*
      *chiel-a-o rech

  b) Modal auxiliaries always precede head verb.
      nyaka a-chiel rech   *I must fry fish*
      a-chiel-o nyaka rech   *I also fry fish*
      *a-chiel-o nyaka rech   *I frying must fish*

  c) Negation markers always precede the head verb.
      ok a-chiel-o rech   *I have not fried fish*
      *a-chiel-o ok rech   **I fry not fish*

  d) Tense markers always precede the head verb.
      ne a-chiel-o rech   *I fried fish*
      * a-chiel-o ne rech   **fried I fish*

  e) Negation markers ok can alternate positions with the past tense marker *ne*.
      ok ne a-chiel-o rech   *I did not fried fish*
      ne ok a-chiel-o rech   *I did not fry fish*

  f) Variations in phonological operations yield varied morphosyntactic interpretations.
      a-cheil-o rech: *I fry fish, I am frying fish, I was frying fish, I have fried fish*

3

THEORETICAL ANALYSIS OF PHASE STRUCTURE OF DHOLUO VERB SYSTEM

Structural Design

The diagram below summarizes the structural architecture propagated by Derivation by Phase Theory.

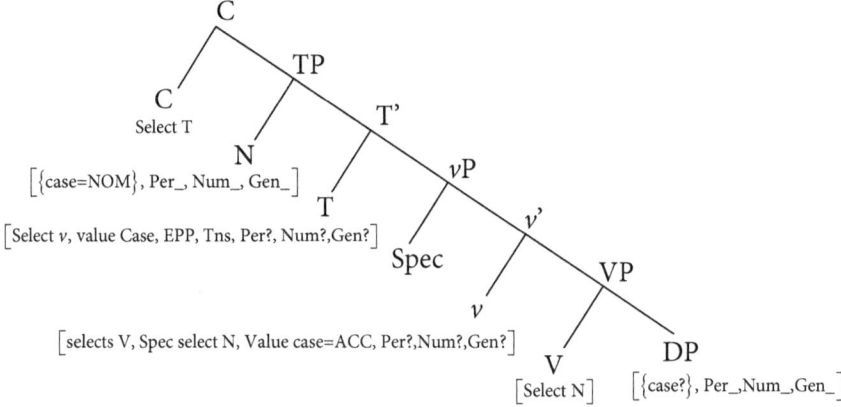

Derivation by Phase theory is based on a probe–goal relationship that is operationalized by the operations Merge and Agree and driven by three Core Functional Categories (CFCs), that is, a light verb (v), Complementizer (C) and Tense projector (T). Chomsky (2000, 2001, 2004, and 2005) argues that in the computation of an Expression (EXP), lexical items (LI) from the lexicon (Lex) enter the derivation processes bearing either interpretable features or uninterpretable features, valued feature or unvalued features. It is the uninterpretable or unvalued features on the probes, that is, the Core Functional Categories that drive the computational process. The C F Cs p r obe for interpretable or valued features available in their goals so that through an Agree operation, such features are valued and deleted. Once these features have been valued, the derivation allows for a transfer process which sends the chunks to the Phonological and semantic components for phonetic and semantic interpretation respectively. Once the probe projects to form a phase, that is, a transitive verb phase (vP) or complementizer phase (CP), the phase becomes impenetrable to other syntactic operation through the Phase impenetrability condition (PIC) and is therefore spelled out.

Radford (2009) points out that structure building operations in Derivation by Phase theory takes place in a bottom–up fashion. THis means that the lower parts of the structural representation build up before the ascending layers. Using the sentence *Robert will fry fish* the structure would build up as shown in the next paragraph.

THe verb (V) *fry* selects and merges with its direct object, a determiner phrase (DP) headed by the Noun *fish* to form the V-bar *fry fish*. THe Noun *fish* enters the derivation with interpretable features Person as third person and number marked as singular but its case is unassigned [Fish{Per=3rd }, {Num=Sg}, {case=?}]. THe transitive verb fry requires an external argument that is an Agent. THe V-bar then projects to merge with the Agent Robert which Fills the Spec–VP to form the expression *Robert fry fish* as illustrated in 63.

63. *Robert Fry Fish*

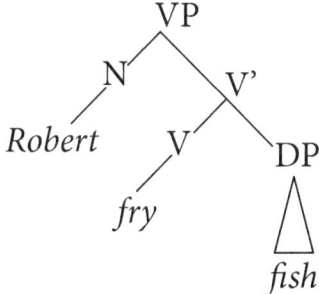

THe VP is regarded as a complement of the light verb *v*. it is the light verb *v* that selects V in the VP projection to Fill the v–bar position. THe light verb c– commands the DP Fish and thus probes it and values its case by assigning it an accusative case. One feature of all Core Functional Categories is the existence of an Extended Projection Principle (EPP) feature. THerefore, the light verb *v* triggers the raising of the subject noun Robert to Fill the vacant Spec–*v* position from spec–VP position. THis process leaves a copy of both the verb from V–bar and the noun from spec–VP. We shall adopt Radford's (2009:325) use of italics to represent copies. THe new structure will be as shown below:

64.

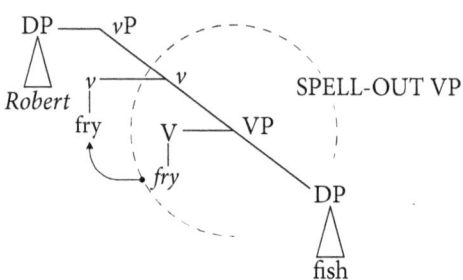

The VP is regarded as a complement of the light verb. It is therefore complete and is transferred to the phonological and semantic component. Radford (2009) posits that the copies do not receive a phonetic representation in the phonological component. For the purpose of tense interpretation on the verb, the *v*P merges with the T–bar which is the head of the tense projection (TP).

The core functional category T represented by the auxiliary verb will enters the derivation bearing an interpretable tense (*i*T) feature. However, the other features person and number are uninterpretable and unvalued. Chomsky (2001) explains that T inherits its features from the complementizer (C). As a probe, T scans and searches for an active goal in its c–command domain. The DP headed by the noun Robert is still active since it has its case unassigned. T therefore agrees and assigns a nominative case on the DP Robert. T-bar projects so as to allow its spec–T position to be filled by the nominative case Robert. The resulting structure forms the phase *v*P and TP projection. *v*P is therefore transferred to the phonological and semantic component. TP remains as a phase boundary in the event that a complementizer was in the expression such as *whether/that Robert will fry fish*.

65.

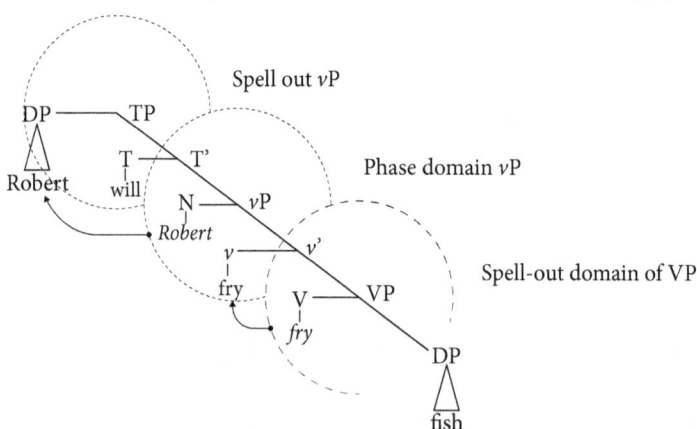

T-Constituent

All the projections that account for tense or aspect interpretations are constituents of the tense projection (TP) (Radford, 2009). As a result, tense probe (T) and Aspect probe (Asp) occupy the T projection in a given phase. Derivation by Phase theory proposes that syntactic computation is driven by probes bearing certain features scanning and searching for a goal bearing certain features in their c-command domain. These features are either interpretable features (iF), uninterpretable features (uF) or unvalued features (unF).

We shall limit our discussion to that of tense and aspect in the TP and leave out syntactic operations such as those involving agreement between T and subject DP in the specifier position in English but not in Dholuo (for chapter 4) and focus on agreement between T-constituents and the finite verb. This bias is grounded on the strict cyclicity principle which allows for selective description of syntactic operations that usually occur simultaneously. The principle states as follows.

66. Strict Cyclicity Principle(Radford, 2009:40)

At a stage of derivation where a given projection HP is being cycled or processed, only operations involving the head of HP and some other constituent c-commanded by H can apply.

Tense in Dholuo

Tense marking in Dholuo involves an agreement between the tense probe T and the finite light verb v in the vP bar. Dholuo marks tense in three different ways. Present tense is marked by a null tense marker {Ø}, past tense is marked by a particle {*ne*} while future tense is marked by the affixal auxiliary {–biro}. This is illustrated in the following sentences.

67. a–med–o pi *I (am adding/add) water*
    1PerSg–add–FV water {Ø} present tense

68. ne a–med–o pi *I added water*
    Pst 1PerSg–add–FV water {*ne*} past tense

69. a–biro med–o rech *I will add water*
    1PerSg–will add–FV water {–biro} future tense

As shown in the examples tense in Dholuo is marked on the tense category and not on the FINite verb while in example 69, tense is marked on the auxiliary verb. THis implies that tense on T bears a valued and interpretable tense [iT, val] and that the FINite verb bears uninterpretable and unvalued tense [uT]. According to the adopted theory in this study, the probe T probes a goal which it c-commands in order to have its uninterpretable features valued. However, in Dholuo, tense as a probe bears interpretable feature of tense [iT] and it is the verb that bears uninterpretable tense feature [uT]. Consequently, the verb cannot probe T because its v does not c-command T.

According to Chomsky's notion of agreement, it is unvalued or uninterpretable features that make a lexical item a probe. However, tense is both interpretable and valued on T in the TP projection. Hence, Chomsky's notion of agree is not sufficient to account for tense and verb relation in Dholuo verb system. Chomsky states

70. Agree as a process of valuation (Chomsky, 2000, 2001)

   i. An unvalued feature F (a probe) on a head H scans its c-command domain for another instance of a F (a goal) with which to agree.
   ii. If the goal has a value, its value is assigned as the value of the probe.

Adger (2002) argues that the kind of agree between the interpretable tense feature on the probe T and the uninterpretable tense features (uT) on the finite verb can only be accounted for via a checking procedure that ensures the interpretable features on **T** are matched with that on v. Once the features are checked, the finite verb will have matching features with T. Matching Features of T in Dholuo means that the verb will bear present, past or future tense. Bejar (2003) echoes similar sentiments by Adger (2002) and explains that the transfer of features from a controller that is a probe to its target, that is a goal, is achieved by syntactic operation of valuation. Elsewhere, Pesetsky and Torrego (2007) offer an alternative approach to account for agree between the probe T and the goal v. In their approach, agreement between tense and finite verb is not driven based on interpretability but rather by valuation. They thus add that an interpretable feature like tense on T is able to probe and value an uninterpretable feature tense (uT) on the finite verb as shown in (9):

71. Step 1: T probes and locates v in its c-command domain. $\left[T_{(iT)}\right] \cdots \left[v_{(uT)}\right]$

    Step 2: Tense features in T checked on the tense features in v. $\left[T_{(iT)}\right] \cdots \left[v_{(uT)}\right]$

Step 3: Tense is valued on *v*. $\left[T_{(iT)} \right] \cdots \left[v_{\{uT\}} \text{ val} \right]$

These steps can account for the valuing of tense in Dholuo present tense as well as past tense whereby the tense features on T are matched and valued on the finite verb. Chomsky (2005:13) warns that failure to value the unvalued features in the goal would result in a derivational crush in syntax. Therefore, if the wrong tense is valued to the verb, the result will be an unwanted derivation. Given the nature of subjects being attached on the verb in Dholuo we will assume Chomsky's (1993) assumption that the verb is drawn from the Lexicon (Lex) already inflected and syntactic operations will simply operate on non-phonological heads in the derivation.

The verb *medo* (to add) will enter the derivation already fused with the first person pronoun [a-] to form the verb *amedo* (I'm adding). *Amedo* will merge with its direct object which is the noun *pi* (water). V in VP is then raised by the light verb to form a *v*-bar projection. The *v*-bar projection project to form the *v*P which merges with the tense head T. At this point, VP is a complement of *v* and is thus transferred to the phonological and semantic components. T bears categorical feature of interpretable tense, valued as present tense. T will then probe and scan its nearest goal and match the features to that of the verb which it c-commands. Consequently, the verb *amedo* will be spelled out as having the value of present tense. This is represented in the structure as illustrated in example 72.

72.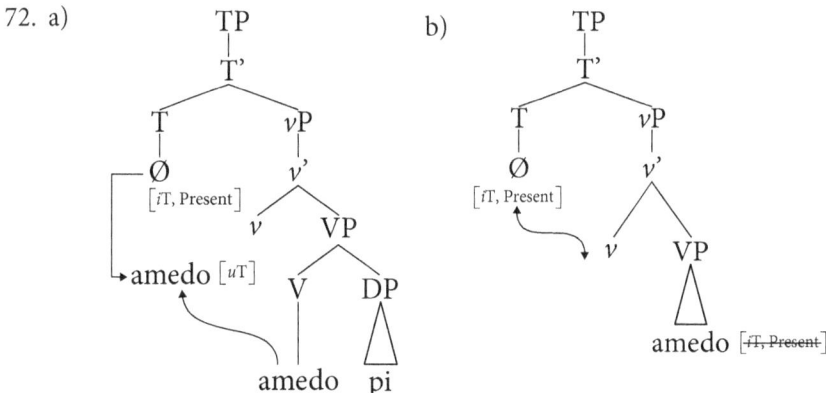

Unlike present tense and past tense which simply imply valuation of tense on the T in Tense projection, future tense in Dholuo uses the future marker and auxiliary verb [*-biro*]. However, *biro* requires a subject to be attached to it and not on the head verb. Below is the generation of the sentence *abiro medo pi* (I will add water):

73. a–biro med–o pi　　　　　　　　　　　*I will add water*
　　1PerSg–will add–FV water

Note that in the adopted theoretical framework, the tense probe T enters in agree relation with the subject of the verb in a specifier head relation. However, there is no Tense and subject agreement in Dholuo so that the subject marker on the modal auxiliary is licensed. We will, however, discuss the notion of tense and subject agreement in chapter four. Future tense will thus be valued by checking and matching the interpretable and valued tense features on the auxiliary verb to the verb in the *v*P phase as shown below.

74. a) …T$[i\text{T: Future}]…v[u\text{T:}\_]\to…T[i\text{T: Future}]…v[u\text{T:}\_]$ **T probes *v***

b) …T$[i\text{T: Future}]…v[u\text{T:}\_]\to…T[i\text{T: Future}]…v[$~~*i*T: Future~~$]$ **T valued on *v***

c) $[\text{T abiro}_{[i\text{T: Future}]}]\,[v\,\text{medo}_{[u\text{T:}\_]}\,[\text{VP…}]]\to[\text{T abiro}_{[i\text{T: Future}]}]\,[v\,\text{medo}_{[\sout{i\text{T: Future}}]}\,[\text{VP…}]]$

Aspect Projection (AspP) in Dholuo

Aspect projection (AP) in Dholuo is headed by preverbal aspect marker {–se} for perfective aspect and the suffix imperfective habitual aspect marker {–ga}. Radford (2009:243) points out that aspect is also interpretable on the aspect head Asp in a similar fashion as tense are interpretable on T.

75. a) a–med–o pi
　　　1PerSg–add–FV water　　　{Ø} perfective/imperfective aspect.
　　b) a–se med–o pi
　　　1PerSg–Asp add–FV water　　{–se} perfective aspect.
　　c) a–med–o–ga pi
　　　1PerSg–add–FV–Asp water　　{–ga} habitual aspect.

We would like to adopt the methodology used by Fukuda (2008) which proposes a high aspect (H–Asp) phrase above the *v*P and a low aspect (L–Asp) phrase below the *v*P. In his analysis, Fukuda posits that a high aspect takes the light verb phrase as its complement while in low aspect; the verb takes aspect as its complement. This information is illustrated in example 76.

76. a) H-AspP   b) L-AspP

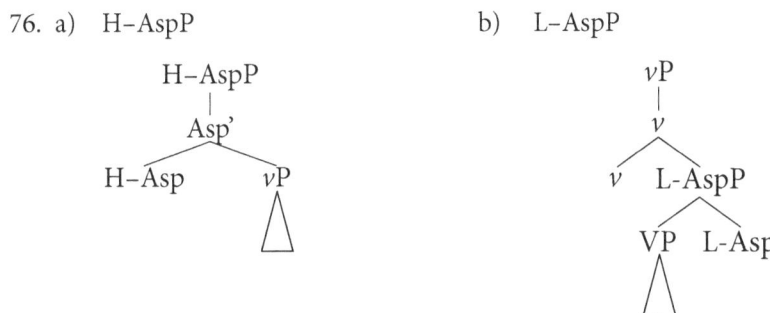

In the derivation of the high applicative as shown above the light verb v-bar is formed and takes VP as its complement. The transitive verb *v* projects its spec-v to form a *v*P bar.it is thereafter that the H-AspP is introduced in the syntax. The H-AspP takes *v*P as its complement and establishes a predicated relation with it. Consequently, H-Asp can probe the *v* which it c-commands in the v-bar and it will value the uninterpretable aspect [unAsp] on the verb.

In the derivation of sentence in *ase medo pi* (I have added water), the high aspect probes the verb which it c-commands. The perfective aspect marker {-se} bears interpretable and valued aspectual features [iAsp: Perf] but the verb bears uninterpretable and unvalued aspect [uAsp:]. Through feature checking and valuing, the probe matches its features on the verb and the features are deleted once valued. As a result, the verb is spelled out bearing a perfective (perf) aspect as shown in (c) below:

77. a) Asp[iAsp: perf]...v[uAsp:_] → Asp[iAsp: perf]...v[iAsp:_] **T probes v**

b) Asp[iAsp: perf]...v[uAsp:_] → Asp[iAsp: perf]...v[iAsp: perf] **T valued on**

c) [Asp ase[iAsp: pef]] [v medo[uAsp:_] [VP...]] → [Asp ase[iAsp: pef]] [v medo[iAsp: pef] [VP...]]

Split Tense Projection

Tense projection in Dholuo can be split to account for both tense and aspect of the verb in the *v*P. This split is motivated by past perfect sentences and the projection is represented below.

78. a) ne a-med-o pi   *I added water*   past tense
       Pst 1PerSg-add-FV pi
    b) a-se med-o pi   *I have added water*   perfective aspect

1PerSg-Asp add-FV water

c) ne a-se med-o pi   *I had added water*   past perfect aspect

Pst 1PerSg-Asp add-FV water

79. Split Tense Phrase Projection

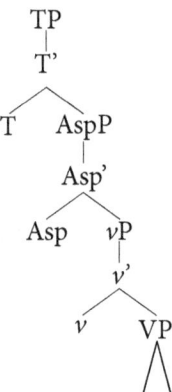

In a split TP, the finite verb enters the derivation bearing interpretable tense [iT] and interpretable aspect [iAsp]. T will probe the verb via long distance agreement and value the tense for the verb as past. Simultaneously, Asp will probe v which it c-commands and value aspect on the verb. As illustrated in example 80.

Tense and finite verb in a long distance agreement

80. $_{TP}$ne $\left[_{AspP} \text{ase} \left[_{vP} \left[_v \text{medo} \left[_{VP} [\text{pi}]\right]\right]\right]\right]$

Aspect and verb agree

Negation in Dholuo

Negation in Dholuo is marked by negation particles {*ok*}, {*kik*} and {*pok*}. {*ok*} is a general negation marker while {*kik*} and {*pok*} are used only in imperative constructions and perfect tense constructions, respectively. According to the classification done by Zanuttini (1998), Dholuo negation marker is a *strong negation marker* in that it can negate a clause on its own without the need of another negation particle; it appears before a finite verb, or an auxiliary verb.

81. a) a-med-o pi   1PerSg-add-FV water   *I am adding water*

	ok a–med–o pi	Neg 1PerSg–add–FV water	$\left[\text{Neg}\left[v\text{P}...\right]\right]$
b)	ne a–med–o pi	Pst 1PerSg–add–FV water	*I added water*
	ok ne a–med–o pi	Neg Pst 1PerSg–add–FV water	$\left[\text{Neg}\left[\text{TP}...\left[v\text{P}...\right]\right]\right]$
	ok ne a–med–o pi	Pst Neg 1PerSg–add–FV water	$\left[\text{TP}\left[\text{Neg}\left[v\text{P}...\right]\right]\right]$
c)	a–med–o pi	1PerSg–add–FV water	
	pok a–med–o pi	Neg Pst 1PerSg–add–FV water	$\left[\text{Neg}\left[\text{AspP}\varnothing\left[v\text{P}...\right]\right]\right]$

Negation in Dholuo is a preverb operation that can take the VP as its complement or take the whole TP as its complement without generating ungrammatical sentences in Dholuo as in (81, b). This free syntactic distribution of the negation marker establishes a parametric variation in Dholuo and is argued for by Omondi (1982) and Okombo (1997). Zeijlstra (2004:177) cites Ouhalla (1991) as having formulated the negation parameter to account for the lack of fixed order in languages as:

82. NEG Parameter

   a) NegP selects TP
   b) NegP selects VP

Zeijlstra adds that a negation element introduces a negative context to the sentence. Therefore, we will treat the value of negation markers as a *negative context value*. The negation marker bears interpretable and feature [*i*Neg] it will therefore probe through the clause to find the finite verb (goal) bearing an uninterpretable negation [*u*Neg]. The negation marker in NegP c–commands the finite verb in the *v*P. Through agree operation the negation is valued.

83. Relationship between NegP and the finite verb

   a) Neg[*i*Neg:Neg context] *v*[*u*Neg:_] → Neg[*i*Neg] *v*[*u*Neg:_] Neg probes v
   b) Neg[*i*Neg:Neg context] *v*[*u*Neg:_] → Neg[*i*Neg:Neg context] *v*[~~*i*Neg:Neg context~~] Neg valued on v
   c) [Neg ok[*i*Neg:Neg context]] [*v* medo[*u*Neg:_]] [VP...] → [Neg ok[*i*Neg:Neg context]] [*v* medo *v*[~~*i*Neg:Neg context~~]] [VP...]

Summary

The tense probe in Dholuo does not need to probe the specifier position of the light verb to enter and agree with the subject because there is no relationship between tense and subject in Dholuo. This chapter has shown that tense and aspect are interpretable and valued on the probes and therefore the only motivating factor of them being probes is not interpretability but rather valuation of their goal, the verb. The chapter has also pointed out the flexible nature of Dholuo negation in relation to tense and the fact that Dholuo can also adopt a split projection of the T-constituent. It is important to point out that there are some slight modifications in the theoretical framework so as to account for Dholuo tense, aspect and negation.

4
CASE ASSIGNMENT AND DERIVATIONAL MORPHOLOGY

Case assignment in Derivation by Phase Theory

Structural case assignment in Derivation by Phase theory by Chomsky (2000, 2001) is as a consequence of agreement between the uninterpretable features on the probes and the interpretable features on the goal. The probes that assign case are the tense probe T which assigns nominative case to the subject and the light verb v assigns an accusative case on the object. Chomsky (2001:6) clarifies that case is not a feature or property of the probe but rather an ability of the probes to assign case to their goals. The assumption is that on one hand the goals, that is, subjects or objects enter the derivation bearing complete and interpretable phi-features of person and number while the probes (T and v) bear uninterpretable person number features. Radford summarizes agreement as:

84. Agreement(Radford, 2009:241)

When a probe (like T) agrees with a goal in its local domain;

a) The unvalued (person/number) φ-features on the probe will be valued (i.e. assigned a value which is a copy of that on the goal).
b) The unvalued case features on the goal will be valued (i.e. assigned a value dependent on the nature of the probe- e.g. nominative if the probe is a finite T).

CASE ASSIGNMENT AND DERIVATIONAL MORPHOLOGY

Case assignment in derivation by phase is a four steps procedure that involves matching of features between probes and their goals, followed by valuation of the features, deletion of features that have been valued and consequently, the assignment of case. Pesetsky and Torrego (2004, 2007) argue that bearing in mind Chomsky's probe-goal framework within which case is assigned, then case is simply a '*by-product*' or a '*bonus*' of the operation agree.

The assigning of case to the sentences *I add water* would start by a merging the verb add and the determiner phrase headed by the noun water to form the V-projection adds water. Additionally, the VP will merge with the light verb v which selects V to form the v-bar projection. The v' will then project to accommodate the spec-v slot available due to the EPP feature and form vP. Note that the light verb bears uninterpretable features of person and number while the determiner phrase headed by the noun water bears interpretable features of Pers=3rd, Num=Sg and the pronoun bears interpretable features of Pers=1st , Num=Sg as illustrated below:

85.

```
                    vP
            PRN          v'
             |
             I          v       VP
      [[Pers=1st, Num=Sg][Case?]]
                        v
                        |
                       add
               [[Pers=? Num=?][Case= Acc]]
                                V       DP
                                |       △
                               add     water
                                    [[Pers=3rd, Num=Sg][Case?]]
```

The light verb v probes its goal, the DP in its c-command domain and has it features matched and valued with those in the DP. Chomsky (2008) maintains that once features have been valued, they must be deleted from narrow syntax. He adds that valuation is important because uninterpretable features may cause the syntactic processes to crush. Once the uninterpretable features on the verb are valued, the probe assigns an accusative case to the DP and it is no longer syntactically active. The VP is then transferred to the phonological and semantic component.

Syntactic computation proceeds by merging the vP with a T-constituent of tense. The tense probe T enters the derivation with uninterpretable features [Pers=? Num=?]. The probe T however has the ability to assign nominative case to a goal that is in its c-command domain. T scans for the goal in the spec–v position and has its uninterpretable features valued and deleted. T consequently assigns a nominative case to the pronoun in spec–v. Due to its EPP feature, T triggers the movement of the subject pronoun from spec–v to spec–T. TP then projects and merges with a complementizer projection headed by null C so that the derivation is given a declarative force and then transferred to the phonological and semantic component and later on spelled out. This is illustrated below.

86.

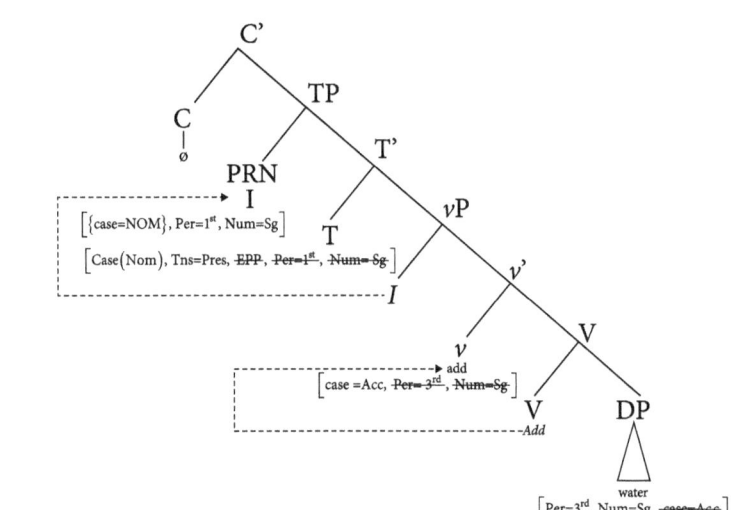

Case assignment in Dholuo

Case assignment in Dholuo is structural case with a nominative and accusative paradigm whereby subjects are nominative and objects are accusatives. Chomsky's (2000, 2001) approach to case assignment is based on the assumption that the tense projection headed by the probe T is a conglomerate of all the features of agree initially separated in the earlier versions of minimalist theory (1995). Chomsky (2005:10–11) points out that the features of T are inherited from the complementizer C. In the earlier versions of Minimalist program, there were Agreement projections that checked the agreement between the verb and its arguments and consequently assign the arguments nominative and accusative case.

The assumption that it is the tense probe T that assigns a nominative case to the subject, external argument to the verb is only probable in English because there is a tripartite relationship between subject–verb and tense inflections in English as would be the case in the third person singular conjugations.

However, Dholuo does not mark different verb forms in relation to subject verb agreement. As a result, to adopt the assumption that it is the tense probe T that assigns a nominative case to the external argument of the verb would be an erroneous generalization. There is however, no contention in adopting the idea that the verb will assign an accusative case to its internal argument in Dholuo. The nature of nominative case assignment in Dholuo is thus best captured by the earlier version of Minimalist program (1995) where the subject was checked by the AGRs (subject agreement projection)

Zwart (2006: 317–339) argues that subject verb agreement is a consequence of structure building operation and not under the control of any functional head. According to Zwart, merging of two syntactic objects, in this case it is the subject and the object is a horizontal affair that doesn't involve any vertical dominance by another functional head. Zwart thus posits that after merge, the subject and the object enter into a sisterhood relationship and that the subject cannot be motivated to check its features with another functional head outside its sisterhood domain.

According to Sigurðsson (2003) structural case assignment is a procedure that simply points out the different attributes of an argument in relation to the verb. As a result, structural case assignment is a sibling correlation between the verb and its arguments. Sigurðsson (2006:289–308) points out that according to Chomsky's (2000, 2001) theory, case is not a feature to be matched between the probe and the goal but rather a feature to be valued. Hence, Sigurðsson argues that there is no need license case through the tense functional head.

Sigurðsson (2006) posits the Low Nominative Hypothesis which argues for the sisterhood correlation between the verb and its argument in case assignment. According to this hypothesis, at the derivation process, the verb will have to decide if it has a participant, i.e. an external argument. If it does, then "… *it gets the Nom value without further ado: it comes for free, is given as the first case.*" p. 297.

Sigurðsson goes on and argue that the second participant, if it is there, will as well get the accusative case without further ado and that the accusative case comes second. This hypothesis can be represented as:

87. The Low Nominative Hypothesis

   a) $V[\theta_1]$ and $(\theta_1 \rightarrow \text{Nom})$

   b) $\theta_2 V[\theta_1]$ and $(\theta_2 \rightarrow \text{Acc})$

   (Sigurðsson, 2006:295)

The idea that case is not licensed and that the Low Nominative hypothesis accounts for how case is assigned can account for the nominative case in Dholuo as well as accusative case. Therefore, in the sentence amedo pi (I am adding water), the assignment of case would be as indicated below.

88. a–med–o pi   *I (am adding/add) water*
    1st Pers– add– FV water

89. a) $V[\theta_1]$ and $(\theta_1 \rightarrow \text{Nom})$
     medo (a–) and $(\{a-\} \rightarrow \text{Nom})$
   b) $\theta_2 V [\theta_1 \text{ and } \theta_2 \rightarrow \text{Acc}]$
     pi medo (a–) and $(\{pi\} \rightarrow \text{Acc})$
   c) a–med–o pi
     1st Pers (Nom)– add–FV water (Acc)

Passive constructions

Passives are derived from active sentences whose subjects have been demoted, In Dholuo, passives are marked by the prefixes {i–} and {o–}. Passive verb forms in Dholuo express internal state of the verb, aspect, rather than tense. There is a wide spread assumption in the analysis of passives sentences by linguists such as Chomsky (2000), Gehrke and Grillo (2009), Radford (2009), Collins (2005) among others that in passive sentence constructions, the object of the active sentence becomes the subject of the passive counterpart. Although this assumption may hold waters in the analysis of passives in English and other world languages, it falls–short in the analysis of Dholuo passive sentence.

Passivization in Dholuo is a radical syntactic operation on the active verb form. THe introduction of the passive preFix to the active verb has some signiFicant eFFects that can be summarized as shown in 90.

90. a) If the passive prefix marker is {o–} the active verb form, the active verb form loses its final vowel marker and adopts a perfective aspect. If the passive marker is {i–}, the active verb form retains its final vowel but automatically adopts imperfective aspect.
   b) The external argument (subject) in the active verb form is demoted to a post verbal position where it is headed by a prepositional phrase.

c) The internal argument of the active verb (object) is retained in the object position without moving to occupy the subject position in the passive counterpart.

91. a–chiel–o   rech   I am frying fish/ I fry fish
    1Pers– fry–FV fish
    i–chiel–o rech (gi an)   fish is being fried (by me)
    Pass–fry–FV   fish (by me)

In Derivation by phase theory, passives are not considered as phases by Chomsky (2000. 2001, 2005). Chomsky also adds that passive verb forms are participles which project a functional head PrtP headed by PRT. The participle does not have full set of unvalued phi–features depending on the language in question. Hence, the PRT can either have unvalued number feature or Person feature but not all features as is the case with the light verb v in transitive counterpart. Consequently, PRT cannot check or value case of its argument. As a result, once the object in the transitive verb moves into the subject position in the passive sentence, the auxiliary verb be in the Tense projection (TP) will check its phi–features and value its case as nominative.

While restricting ourselves to the passive, the derivation of a passive sentence such as fish was fried would commence with the passive subject fish originating as the object of the verb fried. The VP– fried fish is merged with the tense projection headed by the auxiliary verb be. The verb probes its c–command domain to have its unvalued phi–features valued. The nearest goal is the DP fish in the internal argument position of the verb. The unvalued features of the auxiliary verb are matched and valued by the goal; a nominative case is assigned by T. Consequently, the auxiliary verb triggers the movement of the DP to its spec–T position to satisfy the EPP feature. THe derivation proceeds as shown in 92.

92. a) [$_{VP}$ fried fish]
    b) [$_T$ was$_{[Per?\ Num?\ Case(Nom)]}$] [$_{VP}$ fried fish$_{[Per=3rd\ Num=Sg\ Case\ (?)]}$]
    c) [$_{TP}$ fish$_{[Per=3rd\ Num=Sg\ \sout{Case\ (Nom)}]}$] [$_T$ was$_{[\sout{Per=3rd\ Num=Sg}\ Case\ (Nom)]}$] [$_{VP}$ fried Ø]

Given that the object in the passive does not rise to occupy the subject position in Dholuo and that there is no auxiliary verb that checks subject verb agreement in Dholuo, it is evident that the adopted theoretical framework cannot sufficiently account for passive construction in Dholuo without some modifications. This is because of the unique nature of passive construction as indicated in number 91. In addition, case assignment in Dholuo passive construction cannot be accounted for via a tense auxiliary verb. We propose that the PRT head in Dholuo is strong and would trigger a V-to-PRT movement so that the verb can acquire the passive prefix marker. V-to-PRT movement is restricted by the Head Strength Parameter which argues that heads with strong features can trigger rising of weak heads in their lower domain. Radford (2009:133-134) illustrates how Early English allowed verb movement to T while modern English restricts such movements. We will not however dwell on Radford's illustrations here.

Another modification to Chomsky's analysis of Passivization is that we would like to argue that in Dholuo, the object that remains in its base generated position will receive a nominative object case by default since case is not license in relation to the Low Nominative Hypothesis by Sigurðsson (2006:295) discussed earlier on. This nominative object case assigned to the object is because the nominative case comes by default on the first theta that the verb merges with. In this case, the passive participle will scan its c-command domain and find the first goal being the DP in the object position and assign it a nominative case. We would like to caution that this nominative case should not be confused with the nominative case assigned in Icelandic languages as discussed by Woolford (2003) and Ussery (2009).

While ignoring the analysis of the post verbal prepositional phrase in the Dholuo passive sentence in number 91, We propose that in the derivation of the passive sentence ichelo rech (fish is being fried) would proceed as follows: the verb chielo (to fry)will merge with its direct rech to form the VP achielo rech (I am frying fish) the VP will project to merge with the PRT which by virtue of being a strong head, will trigger the movement of the verb to PRT so that it can pick the passive prefix marker. Consequently, the head PRT will radically alter the syntactic features of V and demote the agent to a peripheral phrase to obtain the phrase ichielo rech. PRT will scan its domain for an active goal and find the DP rech and because this is the first goal, it will be assigned a nominative case in the object position, hence the name nominative object case. PRT will project to form the PrtP so that it can project for an aspect phrase (AspP) headed by Asp. The aspect head will value aspect on PRT so that the passive participle is spelled out in an imperfective aspect.

93. a) $\left[_{VP} \text{ achielo rech} \right]$
    b) $\left[_{PRT} \varnothing \{-i\}_{[Per?\ Num?\ Case\ (Nom)]} \right] \left[_{VP} \text{achielo rech }_{[Per=3rd\ Num=Sg\ Case\ (?)]} \right]$

c) $\left[\text{PrtP} \varnothing \left[\text{PRT}\{i-\} \left[\text{VP} \textit{achielo rech}_{[\text{Per=3rd Num=Sg Case (?)}]} \right] \right] \right]$

d) $\left[\text{PrtP} \varnothing \left[\text{PRT} \textit{ichielo}_{[\text{Per?Num?}]} \left[\text{VP} \textit{achielo rech}_{[\text{Per=3rd Num=Sg}]} \right] \right] \right]$

e) $\left[\text{PrtP} \varnothing \left[\text{PRT ichielo}_{[\sout{\text{Per=3rd Num=Sg}}]} \left[\text{VP} \textit{achielo rech}_{[\text{Per=3rd Num=Sg}]} \right] \right] \right]$

f) $\left[\text{AspP} \left[\text{Asp} \left[\text{PrtP} \left[\text{PRT} \{\textit{ichielo}\}_{[\sout{\text{Per=3rd Num=Sg}}]} \left[\text{VP} \textit{achielo rech}_{[\text{Per=3rd Num=Sg}]} \right] \right] \right] \right] \right]$

Antipassive constructions

Antipassive sentences in Dholuo are marked by changing internal word form of the transitive verb root or by a change in tone. The transcription for the verbs in (94) is illustrated in section 2.3.3.

94. a) Antipassives marked by internal word change

English	Transitive form	Antipassive form
To drink	madh–o	metho
To arrange	pang–o	pengo
To get	yud–o	yuto
To open	yaw–o	yepo
To eat	chamo	chiemo
To pay	chul–o	chudo
To fry	chiel–o	chiedo
To boil	chwak–o	chweko

b) Antipassives marked without morphological change to the verb root include:

English	Transitive form	Antipassive form
To peel	pok–o	poko
To remove	gol–o	golo

Antipassives in Dholuo are considered intransitives just like they are considered cross linguistically. However, in Dholuo antipassives, the object of the antipassive verb form is not demoted to a peripheral position but rather it is deleted and its introduction into the antipassive construction bears an ungrammatical sentence as shown in (c).

95. a) a–madh–o chai   (transitive)   *I am drinking tea*
    1Pers–drink–FV tea
    b) a–metho   (antipassive)   *I am drinking*

1Pers–drink (AntP)

c) *a–metho chai   *I am drinking tea*
1Pers–drink (AntP) tea

In the same fashion in which passive sentences in Dholuo are unique from other cross linguistics studies on passives, antipassives are also unique. Linguistic analyses of antipassives by various approaches seem to fall short in the analysis of Dholuo antipassive constructions. Analysis by Aldridge (2012, 2005, and 2004) and Basilico (2003) seem to only cater for languages in which the antipassive object is demoted to a peripheral function while in Dholuo, the object is completely deleted. This radical nature of Dholuo antipassive can be summarized as:

96. a) The transitive verb undergoes internal word change either morphologically or tonally.
    b) The object in the transitive verb is deleted in the antipassive construction and that its inclusion in the antipassive sentence yields ungrammatical sentence.

Despite the lack of cross linguistic support to account for analysis of antipassives in Dholuo, we would like to propose modifications to the adopted theory so as to account for antipassive constructions. We propose that the antipassive verb projection (AntP) headed by an antipassive head (Antp). The Antp head has strong feature licensed by the Head Strength Parameter. As a result, the Antp is able to trigger the rising of the transitive verb in the VP position and radically change it to become antipassive. The merging of the Antp head and the VP projection deletes the object in VP. This deletion violates what Chomsky (2005) refers to the No Tampering Condition (NTC).

97. No Tampering Condition

Merge of X and Y leaves the two SOs unchanged…Merge cannot break up X or Y, or add new features to them. (Chomsky 2005:5)

Chomsky is however lenient on NTC by adding that the condition can be violated if there is a strong principled reason that can still satisfy the Strong Minimalist Thesis (SMT) proposed in Derivation by Phase.

We further propose that the functional head Ant is strong enough to assign a nominative case to the subject it is fused with. The case is assigned as per the Low Nominative Hypothesis proposed by Sigurðsson (2006:295). In addition, the antipassive predicate does not have any phi–features at all. If it had unvalued features, there is no goal to value its features in the derivation.

In the derivation of the antipassive sentences ametho, the transitive verb will merge with its object to form the verb phrase amadho chai the VP will project to merge with the antipassive verb head Antp which will trigger its rising and subsequent radical syntactic changes. The now antipassive verb will project to merge with the tense probe T which will value its tense as present tense. Up to now, the construction is still not a complete phase. The Probe T will then merge with a null complementizer so that the antipassive verb phrase becomes a phase. It will be transferred to the semantic and phonological components for interpretation and spell out.

98. a) [$_{VP}$ amadho chai]   **Transitive VP**

   b) [$_{Ant}$ [$_{VP}$ achielo rech]]

   c) [$_{AntP}$ ∅ [$_{Ant}$ ametho [$_{VP}$ amadho chai]]]   **Rising V to Ant**

   d) [$_C$ [$_{TP}$ [$_T$ [$_{AntP}$ [$_{Ant}$ ametho [$_{VP}$ ~~amadho chai~~]]]]]]   **C phase is spell out**

   Tense probe

Applicative constructions—the Benefactive

Applicatives are argument increasing operation in a language argument structure. Dholuo benefactive applicative is marked by the inflectional suffix marker {-n-} which inflect for object marking. Detailed studies on applicative construction by Pylkkänen (2008) posit that there are two types of applicative; high applicative (HApp) and low applicative (LApp). The high applicative establishes a relationship between an individual and the event being described by the predicate while the low applicative generates a semantic relationship between two arguments of the predicate.

With limitation to the derivational morpheme benefactive, it is worth mentioning that Dholuo benefactive relation is marked either by the benefactive morpheme marker merged on the verb in the event that the beneficiary is pronoun or as a prepositional phrase associated with the verb in the event that the beneficiary of the actions of the predicate is a proper noun below:

99. a) o–chiel–o–n–wa rech   *He is frying fish for us*
       3rd Per Subj–fry–FV–Ben–1 PersPl fish (IO)

   b) o–chiel–o rech ne Robert   *He is frying fish for Robert*
       3rd Per Subj–fry–FV fish (DO) for Robert (IO)

In the passive and antipassive constructions, the benefactive marker remains attached to the verb. In the passive form, the subject is demoted in the construction and the two objects are retained in their base generated positions. In the antipassive construction, the benefactive remains in the suffix position.

100. a) o–chiel–n–wa rech   *fish is fried for us (Perfective)*
     Pass–fried–Ben–1PerPl fish (IO)

   b) chiedo–n–wa   *(expletive/is) frying for us (Perfective)*
     Ant–frying–Ben–1PerPl

Chomsky (2000, 2001) does not discuss the analysis of applicative constructions. We therefore turn to McGinnis (2001 and 2005) who extensively discusses applicative constructions. In here analysis, McGinnis (2000, 2001, 2005) proposes that high applicatives are phases but low applicatives are not. McGinnis (2001, 2005) proposes that phasal applicative have a functional head that may optionally have an EPP feature. The role of the EPP is to attract the lower argument to its specifier position. She proposes that the applicative can be below the VP or above the VP. When the applicative is above the VP it is an E–Applicative and the applied argument, which is, the indirect object (IO), will c–command the theme in the argument, the direct object (DO) as shown in the next page.

101. a) E–applicative   b) I–applicative

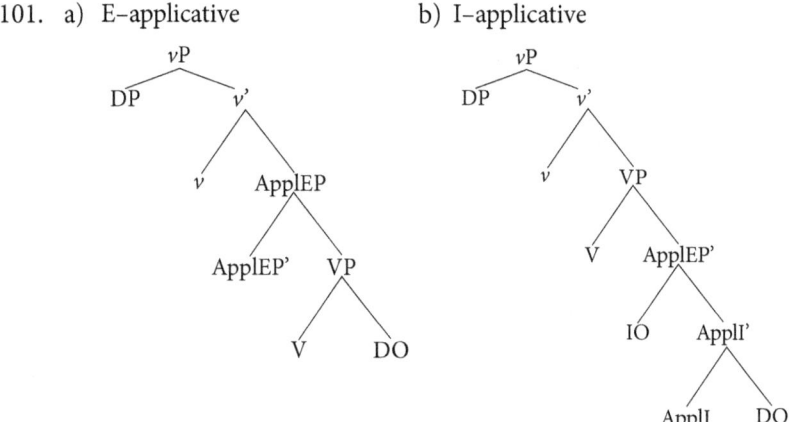

In her phase based analysis of applicatives McGinnis (2000) posits that in an E–applicative, the applicative head is a phase and that it takes the VP as its complement while in an I–applicative, the light verb heads the phase and the applicative head is a complement of V. as a complement of V, the applicative is a merge of both the direct and indirect object.

McGinnis's approach to applicatives seems to bear close resemblance to that of Dholuo, especially the I–applicative. However, we need slight modifications on her proposed structure so as to cater for applicative construction in Dholuo. Firstly, we propose the abolishment of EPP features on the head projections because they are not necessary in Dholuo syntax. Secondly, we propose that once the Applicative projection (ApplIP) loses its EPP feature, the Applicative head (ApplI) is split to cater for the inflectional properties of Dholuo benefactive morpheme. This split of the applicative head will create a sisterhood relationship between the benefactive morpheme and the object which is licensed by the benefactive as an indirect object. The figure is illustrated below.

102. Dholuo I–Applicative

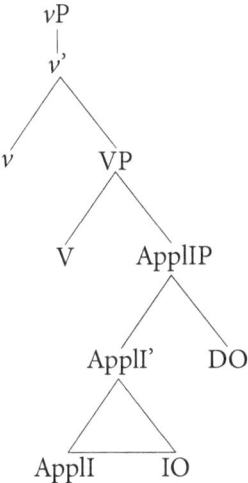

The modifications on McGinnis's structure can accommodate both transitive and intransitive, passives and antipassive sentences in Dholuo. In the event of a passive applicative structure the direct object (DO) remains in tis base generated position while in an antipassive sentence, the DO is deleted altogether and the verb V only takes the applicative head as its complement. The example below will be derived as follows:

103. a–chiel–o–n–i rech   *He is frying fish for us*
      1st Pers Sg Subj–fry–FV–Ben–2nd Pers Sg$_{(IO)}$ fish$_{(DO)}$

The verb V will merge with the applicative head already bearing the affix of the indirect object and separately the direct object to form the VP projection.

The VP projection will merge with the light verb which selects V and triggers its raising to v position. The light verb will then project and merge with a T-constituent, in the case of present tense it will merge with a T and in the case of aspect it will merge with an aspect head so as to check and value either tense or aspect of the verb. Finally, the structure is merged with a null complementizer to have a declarative force. The derivation is shown in example 104.

104. a) $[_C \emptyset [_{TP} T [_{vP} v [_{VP} V [_{ApplP} [_{Appl} IO] DO]]]]]$

b) **Merge applicative with VP**
$[_C \emptyset [_{TP} T [_{vP} v [_{VP} achielo [_{ApplP} [-n-i] rech]]]]]$

c) *v* **selects V**
$[_C \emptyset [_{TP} T [_{vP} v [_{VP} achieloni [_{ApplP} [-n-i] rech]]]]]$

d) **T probes, values tense on V**
$[_C \emptyset [_{TP} T [_{vP} achieloni [_{VP} achieloni [_{ApplP} [-n-i] rech]]]]]$

e) *v***P phase is spelled out**
$[_C \emptyset [_{TP} T [_{vP} achieloni [_{VP} achieloni [_{ApplP} [-n-i] rech]]]]]$

Summary

This chapter has shown that the assumption in the Derivation by Phase theory that there exists a relationship between tense and subject in the assignment of a nominative case cannot hold in Dholuo verb system. We have shown that Dholuo lacks a tripartite relationship of tense–subject–verb and thus assignment of a nominative case requires significant modification on case assignment as opposed to the theory. Given that Derivation by Phase theory is an economic theory, there is no need to renegade back to the introduction of Agreement Projection (AGRs) but rather we adopt a sisterhood correlation proposed by Sigurðsson (2006). This chapter has also shown that Dholuo passives and antipassive constructions behave differently from the proposed approaches in Derivation by Phase theory. For instance the chapter has shown that in passives, the object remains in situ while in antipassives the object is deleted and cannot be added as a peripheral argument.

5
RESEARCH FINDINGS, CONCLUSION AND RECOMMENDATIONS

Research Findings

The research found that the Dholuo verb system has typical phase structure as proposed by Chomsky (2000, 2001). However, it was clear throughout the analysis that Derivation by Phase theory could not in totality account for various variations in the Dholuo verb system in relation to the proposed Probe–Goal framework which reduced syntactic operations to Merge and Agree. The study re-affirms the applicability of the bottom up fashion to structure building operation suggested in the theory. The bottom up fashion is able to account for the relationship between the head verb in Dholuo and its preverbal elements of tense and aspect.

In relation to the **T**-constituents, this study found out that Chomsky's (2000) proposal of merging all functional heads to a **T** probe proposed in the earlier version of Minimalist program (1995) had some challenges when applied in Dholuo verb system. According to Chomsky, uninterpretable and unvalued features act as probes. However, the tense head in Dholuo bears interpretable and valued features and thus cannot be a probe. To ameliorate the situation, we had to turn to Adger (2002), Bejar (2003) and Pesetsky and Torrego (2007) modifications to the probe nature of **T** so as value tense on Dholuo verbs through a valuation condition rather than interpretability condition. Although their approach can account for tense assignment, it does not account for Dholuo subject marker because their analysis is based on the subject and tense relationship which is unique in Dholuo.

Another aspect of the T–constituent that proved difficult to adopt in the analysis of the phase structure in the Dholuo verb system was the assumption that case assignment is a feature licensed by the probes **T** and *v* where nominative case is assigned by **T** and accusative case is assigned by v. the study shows that the accusative case can be assigned by the light verb and feature based syntax proposed in the theory is applicable to account for assignment of accusative case. On the other hand, the assignment of the nominative case could not be licensed by **T** in Dholuo because there is no tripartite relationship between tense head (**T**) and subject–verb agreement as expressed in English. We therefore concluded that **T** cannot assign case in Dholuo. To help us account for case assignment, we had the option of partially adopting Chomsky's approach to assigning accusative case and abandon the nominative case method, or altering the operations involved in case assignment. We opted for the latter and adopted Sigurðsson's (2006) Low Nominative Hypothesis. The challenge of adopting Sigurðsson's hypothesis is that it does not account for the nature of tense in the correlation.

Antipassives and passives are not regarded as phases by Chomsky (2000, 2001). He therefore leaves their analysis as a peripheral affair. In the event that passive constructions are discussed by Chomsky or Radford (2009), the analysis cannot account for Dholuo passive constructions. The assumption in the theory is that passive subjects are generated as objects of the active verb and will be raised to occupy spec-**T** during the syntactic operations. This study showed that such an analysis cannot be used in Dholuo passives because the subject of the active construction is demoted to a post verbal position and the internal argument to the verb is retained in the object position. In the analysis of antipassives, the assumption in the theory is that the internal argument of the verb is demoted to a peripheral position. However in Dholuo, the internal argument of the verbs is not demoted but rather deleted and its re–introduction in the syntax (be it a peripheral position or not) yields an ungrammatical structure. The study showed that even cross–linguistic analysis of antipassives done by Aldridge (2012, 2005, 2004) and Basilico (2003) using Derivation by Phase theory could not account for antipassives in Dholuo.

This study confirmed the hypothesis that Dholuo benefactive morpheme is indeed a low applicative. Chomsky (2000, 2001) does not discuss applicatives in his analyses. Therefore, with slight modifications, this study relied on linguists such as Pylkkänen (2008) and McGinnis (2001 and 2005) who have employed derivation by phase theory in cross linguistics analysis of applicatives.

On the nature of the overall structure of Dholuo verb phase, this study found it difficult to adopt the proposed general structure that advocates for an EPP feature on probes. Chomsky's proposal that probes T, *v* and C bear EPP features is highly applicable to languages like English which have separate, uninflected subjects and objects in relation the verb. In Dholuo, it is impractical to have EPP feature on the verb and other probes because when a feature is to be inserted in the edge of a phase head, the whole verb will have to rise to join the specifier position of the phase head. The edge features therefore had to be deleted altogether because it is redundant in Dholuo verb syntax. On the contrary, the EPP feature can only be retained if and only if there is evidence to show that it can trigger the raising of the verb which has the subject affix to it as well to a specifier position.

This study found out that there was always an attempt to renegade back to the earlier version of Minimalism Theory (1995) whereby the verb with all its inflections would move into various functional head, agreement heads to have its features checked. However, due to the economic and optimal nature of the adopted theory, introduction of such heads as subject agreement head would prove to be uneconomical and non-optimal.

Conclusion

Derivation by Phase theory is a theory that champions for optimality in computational processes involved in deriving an expression. The proposal that language is an optimal solution to its own internal mechanisms involved in derivation is a good assumption towards the understanding of how language analysis and language itself can evolve and be so efficient and effective. There is however a need for a theory that not only reflects the optimal nature of syntactic operation but also mirrors the universal nature of languages as well as various parametric variations. Derivation by phase theory has thus proven significantly that as much as linguists are on the path to narrowing down universal syntactic operations across languages, parametric variations remain to be the pinnacle of any linguistic research.

Recommendation

This study was mainly limited to the analysis of temporal elements such as tense and aspect as well as negation, applicative construction, passives and antipassives. We would like to recommend the following areas for further investigations using Derivation by Phase theory:

1. An account of the determiner phrase in Dholuo.
2. A further study on the assignment of case in Dholuo.
3. Analysis of Wh-constructions in Dholuo.
4. Analysis of Dholuo Clause structure e.g. relative clause and adverbial clauses.
5. Cross-linguistic analysis of derivation by phase between Dholuo (a Nilotic language) and another Bantu language.
6. A significant modification of Derivation by phase theory so that it consistently and fully caters for the parametric variations in Dholuo.

BIBLIOGRAPHY

Adger, D. (2002). *Core Syntax: A Minimalist Approach.* Oxford: Oxford University Press.

Aldridge, E. (2004). *Ergativity and Word Order in Austronesian Languages.* PhD Dissertation Cornell University.

Aldridge, E. 2005. Antipassive, Clefting, and Specificity In Arunachalam, S., Scheffler,T., Sundaresan, S., Tauberer, J. (Eds.), *Penn Working Papers in Linguistics.* Vol. 11.1: Proceedings of the 28th Annual Penn Linguistics Colloquium.

Aldridge, E. (2012). *Antipassive and Ergativity in Tagalog.* Lingua 122:192–203

Basilico, D. (2003). *The Antipassive: Low Transitivity Objects, Syntactic Inertness, and Strong Phases.* Paper presented at the North American Syntax Conference. Montreal: Concordia University.

Bejar, S. (2003). *Phi-syntax.* Doctoral Dissertation. University of Toronto.

Boeckx, C. and Kleanthes, G. (2007). *Remark: Putting Phases in Perspective.* Syntax 10, 204–222.

Booij, G. (2005). *The Grammar of Words: An Introduction to Linguistic Morphology.* Oxford: Oxford University Press.

Chomsky, N. (1957). *Syntactic Structures.* The Hague: Mouton.

Chomsky, N. (1965). *Aspects of the Theory of Syntax.* Cambridge, Mass.: MIT Press

Chomsky, N. (1981). *Lectures on Government and Binding.* Dordrecht: Foris

Chomsky, N. (1995). *The Minimalist Program.* Cambridge, Mass, MIT Press.

Chomsky, N. (2000). Minimalist Inquiries: The Framework. In R. Martin, D. Michaels, & J. Uriagereka (Eds.). *Step by Step Essays on Minimalist Syntax in Honour of Howard Lasnik.* Cambridge, Mass.: MIT Press, 89–155.

Chomsky, N. (2001). Derivation by Phase. In M. Kenstowicz (Ed.). *Ken Hale: A Life in Language.* Cambridge, Mass.: MIT Press, 1–52.

Chomsky, N. (2004). Beyond Explanatory Adequacy. In A. Belletti (Ed.). *Structures and Beyond: The Cartography of Syntactic Structures, Vol 3.*

New York: Oxford University Press, 104–131.

Chomsky, N. (2005). Three Factors in Language Design. *Linguistic Inquiry* 36: 1–22.

Chomsky, N. (2007). Approaching UG from Below. In U. Sauerland & H. M. Gärtner (Eds.). *Interfaces + Recursion = Language? Chomsky's Minimalism and the View From Syntax-Semantics*, Berlin: Mouton de Gruyter, 1–30.

Chomsky, N. (2008). On Phases. In R. Freidin, C. P. Otero, and M. L. Zubizarreta (Eds.), *Foundational Issues in Linguistic Theory: Essays in Honor of Jean-Roger Vergnaud*, Cambridge, Mass.: MIT Press, 133–166.

Cohen, D.W. (1974). The River-Lake Nilotes from the Fifteenth to the Nineteenth Century. In: B. A. Ogot and J. A. Kieran (Eds.). *Zamani: A Survey of East African History*. Nairobi: Longman Kenya.

Collins, C. (2005). A Smuggling Approach to the Passive in English. *Linguistic Inquiry*. 36: 289-297

Comrie, B. (1976). *Aspect: An Introduction To The Study Of Verbal Aspect and Related Problems*. Cambridge: Cambridge University Press.

Fukuda, S. (2008). *Aspectual Verbs and the Aspect Phrase Hypothesis*. Department of Linguistics UCSD. UC San Diego.

Gallego, A. J. (2010). *Phase Theory*. Amsterdam: John Benjamins.

Gallego, A. J. (2007). *Phase Theory and Parametric Variation*. PhD. Dissertation. Universitat Autonoma Barcelona.

Gehrke, B. and Grillo, N. (2009). How to Become Passive In Kleanthes G. (Ed.). *Exploration of Phase Theory: Feature, Arguments and Interpretation at the Interfaces*. Hague: Mouton de Gruyter.

Haspelmath, M. and Sims, A.D. (2010). *Understanding Morphology*. London: Hodder Education.

Haegeman, L. (1994). *Introduction to Government & Binding Theory*. Oxford: Blackwell.

Haegeman, L. (2006). *Thinking Syntactically*. Oxford: Blackwell.

Legate, J.A. (2003). Some Interface Properties of the Phase. *Linguistic Inquiry*, 34(3), 506–516.

Keenan, E. L. and Dryer, M. S. (2007). Passive in the World's Languages In T. Shopen (Ed.). *Language Typology and Syntactic Description*. Vol 1: Clause

Structure. Cambridge: CUP. 325–361.

Ladefoged, P. and Johnson, K. (2011). *A Course in Phonetics*. Wadsworth: Cengage Learning.

Levinson, S. C. (2006). Deixis. In L.R. Horn and G. Ward., The Handbook of Pragmatics. Oxford: Blackwell Publisher.

Lieber, R. (2009). *Introducing Morphology*. Cambridge: Cambridge University Press.

Lyons, J. (1968). *Introduction to Theoretical Linguistics*. Cambridge: Cambridge University Press.

McGinnis, M. (2001). *Variation in the Phase Structure of Applicatives.Linguistic Variation Yearbook*. 1:105–146.

McGinnis, M. (2005). UTAH at Merge: Evidence from multiple Applicatives. In MITWPL 49: *Perspectives on Phases*. M. McGinnis and N. Richards (Eds.). 183–200. MIT Working Papers in Linguistics

Marantz, A. (1997). No Escape from Syntax: Don't Try Morphological Analysis in the Privacy of Your Own Lexicon. In A. Dimitriadis, L. Siegel, et. al., (Eds.). *University of Pennsylvania Working Papers In Linguistics*, vol. 4.2, Proceedings of the 21st Annual Penn Linguistics Colloquium, 1997, pp. 201–225.

Ochieng, J. A. (2012). *Dholuo sub-dialects : Dialectical Variations within Boro-Ukwala Dialect*. M. A. Thesis: University of Nairobi.

Ochola, E.A. (2003). *A Morphosyntactic Analysis of Dholuo Verbal System*. Unpublished MA Dissertation, University of Nairobi. Nairobi.

Odhiambo, J. H. A. (1981). *Dholuo phonology: A Study of the Major Vowel Processes*. MA Dissertation, University of Nairobi. Nairobi.

Oduor, J. A. N. (2002). *A Study of Syllable Weight and Its Effects in Dholuo Phonology*. Unpublished Ph.D. Dissertation, University of Nairobi. Nairobi.

Oduol, J. H. O (1990). *Dholuo Dialects Synchronic State and Some Historical Inferences*. Ph.D. Thesis: University of Nairobi.

Okombo, O. D. (1997). *The functional paradigm and Dholuo constituent order*. Unpublished PhD Dissertation, University of Nairobi. Nairobi.

Okombo, O.D. (1982). *Dholuo Morphophonemics in a Generative Framework*. Berlin: Dietrich Reimer Verlag.

Oluoch, E. A. (2004). *A Morphosyntactic Analysis of Mood in Dholuo: The Minimalist Programme Approach.* Unpublished MA Dissertation, University of Nairobi. Nairobi.

Omondi, L. (1982). *The Major Syntactic Structures of Dholuo.* Berlin: Dietrich Reimer Verlag.

Pesetsky, D. and E. Torrego (2007). The Syntax of Valuation and the Interpretability of Features. In S. Karimi, V. Samiin and Wilkins, W. K. (Eds.). *Phrasal and Clausal Architecture: Syntactic Derivation and Interpretation*, Amsterdam: John Benjamins, 262–294.

Pesetsky, D. and E. Torrego. (2004). Tense, Case, and the Nature of Syntactic Categories In *The Syntax of Tense*, (Ed.). J. Gueron and J. Lecarme, 495–537. Cambridge, Mass.: MIT Press.

Pylkkänen, L. (2002). *Introducing Arguments.* Doctoral Dissertation, MIT.

Pylkkänen, L., & McElree, B. (2006). The Syntax-Semantics Interface: On-Line Composition of Sentence Meaning In *Handbook of Psycholinguistics* (pp. 539–579). Elsevier Ltd. DOI: 10.1016/B978-012369374-7/50015-8.

Radford, A. (2009). *English Sentence Structure.* Cambridge: Cambridge University Press.

Sigurðsson, H.A. (2006). The Nominative Puzzle and the Low Nominative Hypothesis. *Linguistic Inquiry.* 37(2) 289–308.

Sigurðsson, H. A. (2003). Case: Abstract vs. Morphological. In Ellen B. and Heike, Z. (Eds). *New Perspectives on Case Theory.* Stanford: CSLI Publications. pp. 223–268.

Stafford, R. L. (1967). *An Elementary Luo Grammar with Vocabularies.* Nairobi: Oxford University Press.

Suleh, A. E. (2013). *A Morphosyntactic Analysis of Ambiguity of Mood In Dholuo: The Minimalist Programme Approach (1995).* Doctoral Dissertation, University of South Africa.

Ussery, C. (2009). *Optionality and Variability: Syntactic Licensing Meets Morphological Spell-Out.* Doctoral Dissertation, University of Massachusetts Amherst.

Woolford, E. (2006). *Lexical case, Inherent Case and Argument Structure.Linguistic Inquiry.* 37(1) 111–130.

Woolford, E. (2003). Nominative Objects and Case Locality In *Formal Approaches to Slavic Linguistics: The Amherst Meeting* 2002, Ed. by Wayles

Browne, Ji-Yung Kim, Barbara H, Partee, and Robert A. Rothstein, 539–568. Ann Arbor: Michigan Slavic Publications.

Zanuttini, R. (1998). *Negation and Clausal Structure*. A Comparative Study of Romance languages. Oxford studies in comparative syntax. New York, Oxford: Oxford University Press.

Zeijlstra, H. (2004). *Sentential Negation and Negative Concord*. PhD Dissertation University of Amsterdam. Utrecht: LOT Publications.

Zwart, J.W. (2006). Local Agreement. In Boeckx, C. (Ed.) *Agreement Syntax*. Amsterdam: Benjamins. pp. 317–339

#CFP

Call for Papers

Publish with us! As an international Berlin publisher's house we are offering a professional publishing enviroment. As international scientific book sellers we have more than 30 years of experience in the book market.

You have African or Asian Studies to publish? We are predominately interested in the humanities, arts and law. Works devoted to country or territory specific topics will receive most interest. We do not publish Medical and Scientific works with the exception of endemic studies.

French, German and English manuscripts are welcome. With regard to other languages we offer a professional translation service.

To discuss your proposal please email us at **contact@galda.com** and our editorial team will reply in return.

www.galda-verlag.de

www.ingramcontent.com/pod-product-compliance
Lightning Source LLC
Chambersburg PA
CBHW070833300426
44111CB00014B/2539